MYSTICAL, MAGICAL
MAHARASHTRA

MILIND GUNAJI

Popular Prakashan
www.popularprakashan.com

Published by
Harsha Bhatkal for
POPULAR PRAKASHAN PVT. LTD.
301, Mahalaxmi Chambers
22, Bhulabhai Desai Road
Mumbai 400026
www.popularprakashan.com

First Published 2010
Second Reprint January 2016

(4193)
ISBN 978-81-7991-445-8

Book & Cover Design by Namita Jadhav & Mahendra Ghanekar

Photo Credits
Author on the back cover : Jagdish Mali
Cover : Milind Gunaji
Inside : Milind Gunaji, Swapnil Pawar (Indravajra), Satish Akkalkot,
Dr. Ravi Roopvate, Madhav Fadke
On the Cover : Mochemaad

Translated from Marathi by Reshma Kulkarni

Printed in India
by Saurabh Printers (P) Ltd.
Plot No. 67 A-68, Ecotech, Ext. I
Kasna, Greater Noida-201306 (U.P)

Om Kripa Sindhu Sai Nathaya Namah

I dedicate this book to Bapu, my parents, Rani, Abhishek, my family and friends whose loving support accompanies me on all my journeys.

The spirit of adventure and the explorer in you are traits common to both of us. And that gives me a stronger reason to love your personality. Your books make very revealing and interesting reading. And I admire you as an actor.

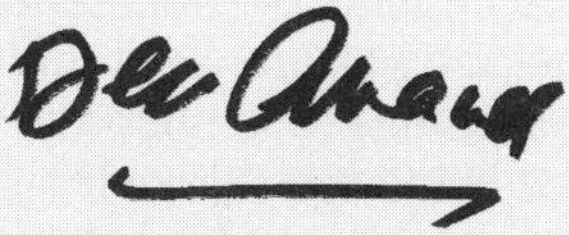

PREFACE

Till now, I have written six books on travel; and my heart fills with joy to say that all my books have received a hearty response from my dear readers. So much so, that the books are now well into their second, third and even the ninth edition, in one case! Not only have my readers enthusiastically welcomed my books; my poems and songs have also received an overwhelming response. In the interim period, Maitreya and Sagarika Music launched 'Man Paakhrache Hoi' – an audio album of my poems and songs. That the audience immensely loved it was evident by the encouraging response to the album via SMSes, emails and letters. But my core remains that of a traveller. Hence, I keep exploring newer and relatively unknown places and write about them in publications such as *Bhatkanti* magazine and *Saamna* newspaper.

It was decided to compile a book of these writings. There are quite a few places in Maharashtra that have remained unexplored by tourists; or have a history of some unique occurrence or have been rumoured to host some mystical phenomenon. *Pedhas* (a kind of sweet used as offering) disappearing at Bhuleshwar, the Chintamani Boulder at Tuljapur moving as per one's wishes when touched by the palms, bubbles arising at a rapid pace in the water at Netravali in Goa as one keeps clapping – these are just some of the examples of the fables connected with some places in Maharashtra. The dome of the temple at Akkalkot devoted to the revered Godman Shri Swami Samartha is said to reverberate with the beats of *mridanga* (a type of drum).

Apart from that, there are many forts with strange names like Narnala, Lalinga, Gaalna etc. Narnala fort is well known for its historical importance coupled with folklore that a man bitten by a dog can get cured at the Shakkar Talav here. The huge footprints of a human being found at Salher add to its charm. So does the two-pronged coconut tree at Sindhudurg, the imprints of Chhatrapati Shivaji Maharaj found in the limestone dome, the wall beneath the sea at Vijaydurg (which was only recently discovered) which used to wreck the enemy ships and cause them to sink in the sea before they could touch the fortress – all of these add to the mystique. Fun facts such as the description of Saamangad where most of the construction has been done underground and mystical facts about certain forts have also been included in this book.

Places such as Amboli and Sindhudurg find a mention in my previous books as well but this book elaborates about them quite a bit. Similarly, readers are bound to like information about Daman, the 'walking mango tree' of Sanjan, the place near Sanjan where Parsis first settled when they came to India, Khaanvel, Silvassa and such other hitherto unknown places. This book will also acclimatize readers with places like the Kaaplingeshwar near Paatpanhala which the Maharashtra government is now developing as a tourist attraction; Gudhe Panchgani, a part of Chandoli which is as beauteous as Mahabaleshwar; Sangli, little-known spots around Kolhapur and so on. Further, the book also contains information about adventure sports started by Chinmay Divekar of Nature Trails and some little-known picturesque resorts.

Many thanks to my friend Nitin Abhyankar for providing valuable information about Bhuleshwar and Kaalbhairav of Gadhinglaj. While I've also clicked photos for the book, it got an additional interesting touch due to the photographs given by my childhood friend, a doctor-cum-trekker, Dr Ravi Roopvate and Madhav Fadke of Chakram Hikers, particularly for the photos of Salher, Saandan, Bahiri and Telbaila.

Similarly, the book has benefitted by some valuable information regarding Sangli and Chandoli, generously provided by Ujjwal Sathe of Chintamani Motors with whom I've come to cement a fantastic friendship in very little time.

Thanks to Pradip Sutar for his photographs of Chandoli and Sagun Bhadkamkar, the developer of Naneghaat for all his inputs about the same.

Satish Akkalkot's superb literature called 'Durg' proved invaluable reference and research material. Ranjit Naik-Nimbalkar gave great information about the Sitabai Mountain.

My heartiest thanks to Varsha Satpalkar and Ajit Acharya of *Bhatkanti* magazine; as also Sanjay Raut of *Saamna* newspaper for allowing me to reproduce my articles in this book.

Also, many thanks to all my friends and my able assistant Anand Acharya. Thanks also to my friend Uddhav Thackeray for his photographs of Vijaydurg and Naldurga. Last but not the least; thanks to my colleague Reshma Kulkarni, for translating the book and also assisting in the drafting of the same.

I'm certain that my readers will welcome this book with as much affection and enthusiasm as they've shown towards my earlier efforts.

Milind Gunaji

CONTENTS

PUNE, SOLAPUR AND NAGAR

1. Khed-Shivapur Dargah

On the Pune-Bangalore highway after the Katraj Ghat, one comes across a village famous for its *dhaabas* (hotels) – Khed Shivapur. Khed Shivapur is also famous for the *dargah* (shrine) of Hazrat Pir Kamarali Durvesh. One feels refreshed to be welcomed into a beautifully maintained shrine with equally good surroundings. It is also amazing to see a boulder weighing 100 kg standing in the compound!

Hazrat Pir Durvesh hailed from Delhi. He came to Pune accompanied by his parents. When Durvesh's brother met an untimely death, he renounced the world to go on the spiritual path. Gaarpir of Pune was his guru. This 745-year old shrine was established by Gaarpir himself. Gaarpir expired in 1235 AD. This shrine used to get Re.1 every year from the British Government as donation – or so the records state!

The boulder has a history of its own. When Lord Indra got angry and showered Gokul with torrential rains, Shri Krishna lifted the Govardhan Mountain on his little finger to give shelter to the people and cattle of Gokul. Taking inspiration, I too tried to lift this 100 kg boulder; I also had 10 more men to assist me! Jokes apart, everyone has to chant aloud the name Kamarali Durvesh whilst trying to lift this boulder. We tried doing this, and believe it or not, we could lift the boulder as if it were a delicate flower – that too, literally with a single finger!

We've also photographed this for *Bhatkanti*. Numerous telly-viewers saw for themselves, how just the eleven of us could lift this huge piece of stone. But there's a scientific theory behind this phenomenon. That is, the Collective Force Theory. Recently a Japanese institute has conducted extensive research on this phenomenon. Abroad, at other places too, the theory is rousing much interest. It is sad to see though, that in India such scientific miracles are still wrapped in the cloak of superstition.

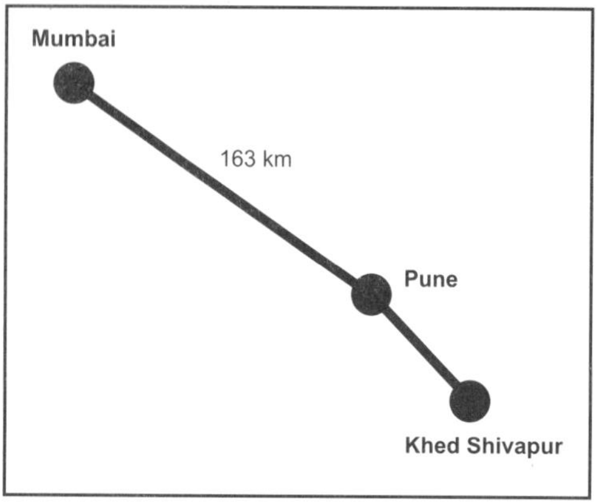

LIFTING THE BOULDER AT THE KAMARALI DURVESH DARGAH

2. Kaanifnath

While going to Saaswad from Pune, there's always the safe route of Diveghaat; but for a change, if you've ever gone via the Baapdev ghaat, you must have noticed a pristine white temple atop a high mountain peak. This is the Kaanifnath temple. Though the mountain seems rocky and aggressive, such mountains are hardly a deterrent for the Marathi *manoos*, who is probably genetically blessed to conquer these and more! The 30-45 minute trek ends before you even realise it. The temple's surroundings are exquisite. The trees provide huge shady canopies, below which a tired trekker can sit on circular stone benches. Besides the main temple, there also are temples devoted to Lord Vitthal, Rakhumai, Kaalbhairav and Datta-paduka.

KAANIFNATH - SAASWAD

At the onset of the monsoon, the surrounding hillocks wrap an emerald cloak around themselves. On one side is the mountain of Diveghaat; on another is Katraj. Far away one can spot the Kedareshwar peak of Purandhar while on yet another side lies bustling Pune city.

The main attraction of this temple is the extremely narrow entrance (9 inch by 11 inch) to the sanctum sanctorum. A tunnel begins from within this rectangular entrance. One has to lie flat on the stomach and try to crawl inside the tunnel to see the Lord. While coming out, one has to crawl back the same way, because it is said that one should not point one's feet to God. A person may be bulky but he manages to crawl inside, provid[illegible] he has faith – or so it is said. In fact, a board at the entrance says [illegible] Shraddha Jyachya Uri, Tyala Dise Kaanifnath Murari" (the God w[illegible] be seen by those who have faith).

The main temple is quite tiny. A route for circumambulating the idol, and the hall have been constructed later. In the hall, are *samadhis* (shrines) of Gorakshnath, Jalindranath and Macchindranath. Festivals like Raamnavmi, Gokulashtami, Dattajayanti and Rangpanchmi are celebrated with fervour. Every full moon day, a palanquin of Kaanifnath is specially worshipped.

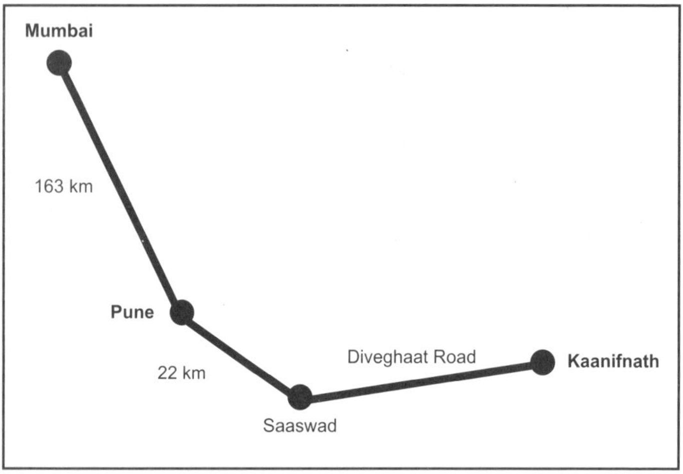

THE NARROW ENTRANCE

3. Diveghaat and Mastani Talav

Utter the words Bajirao and Mastani and a vision of the scandalous love story of a braveheart and a beauty, immediately springs to mind. The love story has become immortal in the history of Peshwas. While going via Diveghaat on the outskirts of Pune city, a pond attracts one's attention; that is the Mastani Talav.

Folklore suggests that this octagonal pond was built by Bajirao Peshwa in honour of Mastani. Bajirao and Mastani used to ride till here on horseback all the way from Pune. Of course, there is no evidence to support these stories but undoubtedly, this dam-like pond and the Ganesh temple nearby, is worth seeing at least once.

The love story of Bajirao and Mastani is one of the legends of Peshwa history.

The best time to go to Diveghaat is when rain is drizzling lightly. We see pictures of Diveghaat overflowing with *waarkaris* (pilgrims) during Ashadh. But it also looks beautiful when towards the end of monsoon, saffron-coloured flowers bloom all over the valley. So engrossed are we admiring the beauty of these flowers enveloping the entire valley that we don't realise when the *ghaat* ends.

4. Green Valley and The Edge

Located in the Pune district, Naneghaat is a picturesque location comprising of tall mountains and deep valleys. In order to reach Naneghaat, drive to Junnar on the Pune-Nasik highway; from Junnar make it to Ghatghar. Alternatively, you can reach Naneghaat via Alephata-Malshej route. If you plan to start from the base of Naneghaat, go upto Murbad from Mumbai via Kalyan. The base of Naneghaat lies along the Murbad-Malshej route very close to Vaishakhare. I reached by car right to the top of Naneghaat. From here unfolds the splendid scenario of the Sahyadri valley. Around the year, a gushing wind keeps you company. During winter and rains the place is engulfed in a blanket of fog.

The historically-prominent Naneghaat is at the base of Fort Jivdhar in Pune district. It is the most ancient route to connect Konkan at sea level to the Deccan plateau which is at an altitude. Naneghaat, the pass, has steps carved out in the mountain 2000 years back by the Satavahana kings to climb down to the Konkan strip from Desh. Desh is the Deccan plateau. We climb down to the base of the ghaat within an hour. The first thing that you see on reaching Naneghaat, is a pot made of stone. You can say this is 'lagaan' dating back 2000 years! In the earlier days, traders plying on this route had to put coins in this pot as octroi. This stone pot, which is an erstwhile toll-booth, has been carved out of a single huge rock. I fancied myself paying toll in the vase and began climbing down.

Along the slope are a few finely carved caves. These caves also date back to the Satavahana period. There are inscriptions in these caves by the Satavahana rulers; especially by queen Naagnika or Nayanika who has described their lineage. Statues of the Satavahana kings and queens once adorned the caves; of which, all we can now see are a few remains.

A huge black rock grabs our attention as we move down Naneghaat. This steep straight rock poses a challenge to hikers. However, by the time I reached there it seemed that a hiker group had pledged to go for it! A proper trainer is all one needs for a safe rappelling of this rock.

A thumb-like projection on the yonder side also holds much fascination and is called Nanacha Angtha (Nana's thumb). I trekked all the way up and stood atop the thumb, 3000 ft above sea level. Words fail to depict the exquisitely beautiful natural landscape in front of me. Here, like a scattered flock of sheep, clouds wander all over the valley. I just feasted my eyes as much as I could, on this grand panorama of nature. Lines of an old romantic poem came alive in my heart as I stood admiring the beauty around. The poem went, "Yonder stands the rock, pitch black and baring its mighty chest, pristine water adding to its glory; Malhar melody glides up the land and valleys; clad in the clouds my mind runs awry!"

There's a fine spot near Nanacha Angtha; it is like a slightly tilted mountainside. From this spot you get a bird's eye view of numerous layers of mountains and valleys in the terrain. I've been to this place numerous times; in fact so many times, that the locals have christened it Gunaji Cliff! Next to Gunaji cliff is the Sagun waterfall. The terrifying sight of the waterfall curdles your blood. There's a peculiar thing about this waterfall; instead of cascading down from high above, it looks as if it flows upwards from down below. This is thanks to the sheer momentum of wind which flows upwards with great force from the valley and pushes water upwards. This wonder of Mother Nature leaves one dumbfounded. This waterfall has been named after Sagun Bhadkamkar, a young and dynamic nature lover and entrepreneur who also loves this waterfall a lot and has developed the whole terrain.

Nowadays the steep peak across Sagun waterfall also attracts visitors in droves. Sometimes one feels like applauding the craftsmanship of Mother Nature. The beautiful peak here reminds you of a naughty boy punished by a teacher, and standing out of the class. The protuberance is called Wandarlingi or Khada Parsi.

All the magic of nature comes alive in the neighbourhood of Naneghaat. On one hand there are lofty cliffs and peaks and on the other, breathtakingly deep valleys. It is here that you find picturesque

NANACHA ANGTHA AT NANEGHAAT

spots to delight you and black rocks to challenge you. Hence, Naneghaat has been gaining tremendous fame as a tourist spot. Being 2500 ft above sea-level and with cool air, a hill station just like Matheran or Mahabaleshwar will soon flourish here. The only hitch in the process of making it a hill station is the final access by road. If you go from Mumbai via Malshej after 8 km, at Madh, the road turns to Junnar via Ganeshkhind. A small bifurcation leads us to Naneghaat. But this 26 km-long road is pretty bad and as a tourist one is tired and bored of this treacherous track and hopes for the journey to end soon. It's good for adventure-oriented people but for regular travel something has to be done about the road.

INSIDE THE SATAVAHANA CAVES, NANEGHAAT

The name of this newly formed hill station is 'The Edge'. Tourism buff Sagun Bhadkamkar has started to develop this plateau. Just for tourists, Bhadkamkar has built a resort, big enough to house 200 trekkers at a time. It's a unique fun to eat and chat with the blowing wind in the background.

Now that we have seen all of Naneghaat plateau, it's time to proceed to the Green Valley at the base. En route from Naneghaat to Green Valley, is Malshej ghaat. This journey too is full of fun for trekkers. The road winds its way though towering cliffs and deep valleys. Jivdan fort, Naneghaat, Malshej ghaat, Lenyadri, Ganesh Leni and Shivneri fort — all these tourist spots are just a stone's throw away from Palu village. However the Green Valley is a full-fledged tourist spot. Here, there's a lake for boating, the thrill of a waterfall, rappelling and jungle trek. It is not possible to organise adventure camps in a city but Green Valley has this facility. It feels great to cross the river hanging upside down from a rope. The deep blue sky high above, a gushing river below and you hanging precariously on a rope, make the perfect ingredients for a great thrill!

There's a natural waterfall in Green Valley which flows in full force even when it's not raining; so, one can simply imagine the force during monsoons! It's great fun getting wet under this waterfall. After having indulged in river crossing, I tried my hand at waterfall rappelling. It was an awesome experience to rappel on slippery rocks through the forceful waterfall. The water falling on my head was hugely distracting but I managed to stay focussed, rappel and successfully climb down into a pool of water.

> *Here, like a scattered flock of sheep, clouds wander all over the valley. I just feasted my eyes as much as I could, on this grand panorama of nature.*

From here I moved ahead to an avenue made for boating. Boats fascinate me; drifting in a boat casting ripples on the placid waters of a lake is a unique experience. My water tour was fantastic; pedalling a boat in the crystal clear waters in lush green surroundings, cheered my mind up immensely. I felt like Columbus exploring a new world! Here in Green Valley, Sagun has a vision to recreate a dense woodland like Amazon. He has begun to develop one part; once the trees grow fully they won't allow even the sunlight to seep through to the earth. This dynamic youth has developed 25 acres of land into a green valley project. Not only does it accommodate small families but also large groups. So, one can say it is a complete family resort. Green Valley caters to veg and non veg patrons alike. Even your special choice of bhakri thecha or a hot spicy mutton curry will be catered to, if ordered in advance.

All in all, one simply cannot give this scenic and beautifully developed locale a miss!

5. Jadhavgadi

The mystery novels of Baburao Arnalkar often describe *gadhis* (mansions akin to small forts). Thus, I had a picture of a *gadhi* painted in my mind as a building having frighteningly squeaky doors that concealed mind-boggling mysteries and secrets. However, when I happened to see a real *gadhi*, called Jadhavgadhi, on the Saaswad road, it was a different sight altogether.

Initially, when I entered, pushing open the towering wooden door to see the dark prisoners' rooms towards my left, I felt my mental picture manifesting itself. But then, on entering inside, when I saw the cannon resting along a wall, a huge courtyard and an imposing stone building, I felt I was seeing more of a historical construction than a mysterious one!

This *gadhi* was built by the braveheart of the Jadhav family, Pilaji Jadhav. Around 300 years earlier, Jadhavrao was going to central India to build a new kingdom. The Peshwas halted him mid-track and thus his dreams remained unfulfilled; else, history would have been written very differently. He built three *gadhis* in all. First, one at Vagholi near Nagar, one at Nanded-Shivne near Pune and lastly at Saaswad. The first two fell to the ravages of time but this one at Saaswad still stands strong.

The *gadhi* stands on a mere 4½ acres today, as opposed to the 40 acres when it was built! Two out of the seven storeys of the *gadhi* are under the ground whereas the rest are above it. From within, the entire *gadhi* is decorated in carved Saagwani wood. The décor of the spacious rooms has a distinctive Mughal style. In the rooms above, that one has to climb narrow stairways to reach, are pictures of kings on a hunting spree, dancers, etc. From the peak of the *gadhi* one can see the whole of Saaswad, Diveghaat and Malharghaat, and faraway farmlands. The *gadhi*, which still has a strong foundation, is looked after by Pilaji's 11th descendant Dada Jadhav. Till 1980, Dada used to stay here. Today he has moved to another place but tourists can see the *gadhi* with his permission. While coming from Pune to Saaswad, Jadhavgadi is located 30 km after crossing Diveghaat.

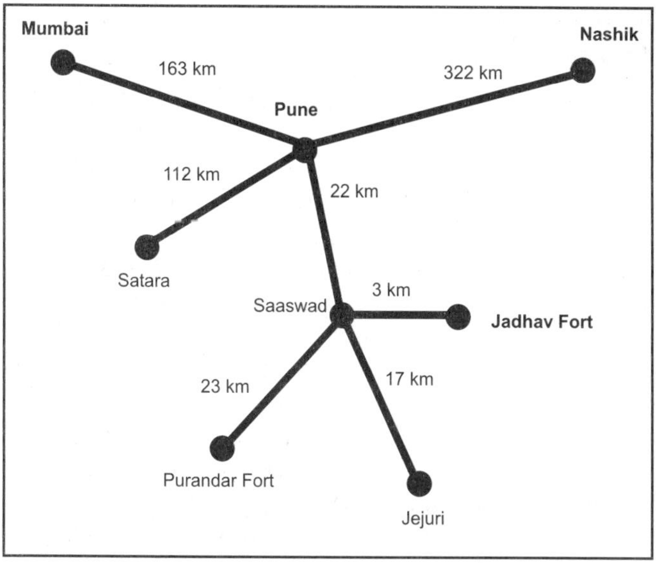

OUTSIDE JADHAVGADI

6. Jejuri

'Deva Tujhi Sonyaachi Jejuri, Gadala Navlakh Paayri'. I had heard these verses umpteen times in Marathi poetry and thus began climbing up those 'navlakh' (nine-lakh) steps to see the temple. At first glance, Jejuri looks like a formidable fort due to its strong protective wall. On crossing the initial few steps and a few stalls selling flowers etc, we come across a statue of Umaji Naik. Umaji Naik had become famed as Robin Hood in the pre-independence days. He had greatly agitated the British with his constant and ingenuous raids on their treasury. A few steps ahead, we see the *deepmaala* (column of lights) and a *mahadarwaza* made of stone. Going beyond this door, one sees a number of tall *deepmaalas*, some of them said to be built by Aurangzeb. The whole place looks yellow due to the turmeric floating around. Outside the temple, one sees the Nandi (bull) and *bagaad* - a stony contraption in front of which devotees ask for their wishes to be granted by Khandoba. The devotees give a feast called *bhandara*, once their wishes get fulfilled. There's a fire-spit below that is constantly on. One has to pour oil in it. There's a statue of Mallasur in the temple's courtyard. There's a folktale associated with this Mallasur. It is said that seven *dharmaputras*, alongwith their wives, had gone to meditate on the Manichurna mountain. They built an ashram on the mountain and began meditating. Soon, a demon called Mallasur, spurred by the power bestowed upon him by a boon from Lord Brahma, came there and destroyed the ashram. The inmates got scared and rushed to Lord Shiva on Kailash Parvat seeking his help. Lord Shiva took the form of Bhairavmartand and killed Mallasur. Thus he came to be known as Malharimartand.

In front of the temple's entrance, is a huge tortoise adorned with a brass sheet with a circumference of 7 m. Rituals like "kali bharna" are done here. In this ritual 5, 7 or 11 people have to touch and lift the *taamhan* (special puja-plate). The *taamhan* contains 5 betel leaves, coins and betelnuts. Then a *bhandara* is given by first flailing fistfuls of turmeric all around. This perennially-crowded temple has idols of Khandoba, Mhalsabai and Banabai.

The surroundings of the temple constantly reverberate with cries of "Yelkot Yelkot Jai Malhar". The idols in the temple have been gifted by Sawai Madhavrao Peshwa and Shahu Maharaj of Kolhapur.The idols of Khandoba and Mhalsabai have been gifted by Chhatrapti Shivaji's step-brother, Vyankoji Raje. It is said that there was a custom wherein if two relatives were meeting after a long time, they had to meet after looking at the reflection of each other's faces in a plate of ghee. It is said that when Shivaji and Shahaji Maharaj met after a long time, they conducted the same ritual over here.

Khandoba's original location is on the Karhe table-land, 2-2 ½ km from Jejuri. There's a folktale associated with why Khandoba came to Jejuri. Apparently, there was a very religious devotee of Khandoba in the family of Kherepatils. For many years till he grew old, he used to come religiously to visit Khandoba at Karhe. One year, due to old age, he fell on the way and couldn't muster the strength to get up and continue the journey. He felt very bad and pleaded with Khandoba to meet him anyhow. Thus Khandoba came to Jejuri, where the man had fallen, and since then, has stayed there itself.

In front of the temple, is a hollow column akin to the *deepmaala.* One can go up this column from within and can have an aerial view of the temple. The crown of the temple is built as per Mughal architecture. There's a Shivlinga up there. It is shut in the rainy season and opened only during Mahashivaratri and Somwati Amawasya. Behind the main temple is a temple devoted to Mhalsa, engraved in stone. Mhalsa was the daughter of a grocer. Khandoba appeared in front of this grocer at Pali and wed Mhalsa on Paush Pournima. Therefore, he is also called as Mhalsakant.

I saw an amusing custom at the Khandoba temple. A groom dressed in formal clothes was carrying his coy, new bride in his arms and climbing up the temple stairs! I later came to know that this is the way a newly-wedded couple goes to meet Khandoba for the first time, to seek his blessings for a happy married life. They need to walk at least 5 steps in this way.

JEJURI

One can see a huge sword here. Its blade is 10 cm broad and a metre long and it weighs 40 kilos! The sword is called Khanda, slayer of all evils (*khandan karne* in Marathi) and hence, one who wields this Khanda is called Khandoba! Every Dussehra, there's a competition to wield this Khanda. I tried it but had to put it down in a second! A brave man once wielded it for 27 minutes!

When I went into the temple, there was a *waghya-murli* folk dance going on. Earlier there was a ritual to give away the first child to Khandoba. If it was a boy, he'd be called Waghya and a girl would be called Murli. However, after the lives of many such Waghyas and Murlis was spoilt due to lack of careful upbringing, the Government banned this ritual. However, the *waghya-murlis* still present here, even today, perform the ritualistic dance of *jaagran* and *gondhal* after any auspicious event.

From the temple's terrace, one can get an amazing aerial view of Jejuri village. You can also see two huge lakes built during the Peshwa reign. The octagonal pond instantly reminds you of the Diveghaat Mastani talav.

Descending the steps behind the temple, one comes to Banabai's shrine. Banabai was Lord Indra's daughter but she grew up at a shepherd's house. Lord Shiva had granted her a boon that she would get any man she desired as her husband. Thus, Banabai chose Khandoba. But Khandoba was already married to Mhalsabai. To solve this puzzle, Khandoba initiated a game of chess with Mhalsabai, with the condition that the one who lost would stay in the forest for twelve

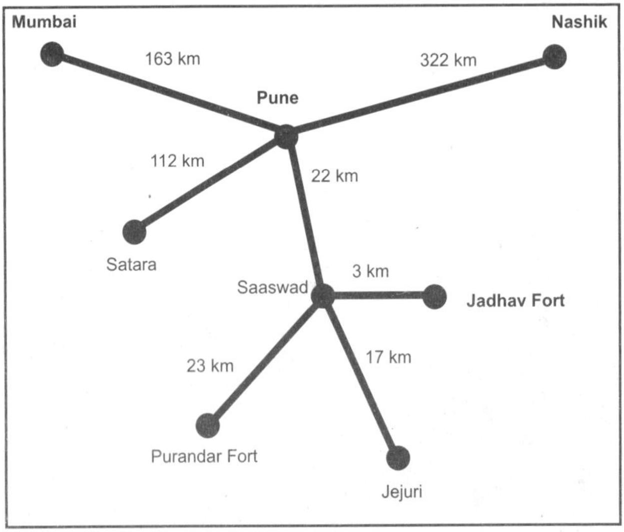

years. Of course, Khandoba lost the game and thus went to stay at the shepherd's house. Later he married Banabai. When he came back with Banabai, Banabai and Mhalsabai just couldn't get along. There's a funny folk song in Marathi, about the two wives' quarrels. It says, "Ya Bai Jejuri Nagrat, Korya Chandni Mahalat, Mhalsa-Banai bhaandti, Aikuni Malhari haasati". Then, Khandoba segregated the fort. He allotted a place to Banabai in the lower part of the fort and would go to meet her every Sunday. Even today, this meeting is commemorated with great pomp each Sunday.

The *kuldaivat* (family deity) of numerous families in Maharashtra, Khandoba is dressed like a warrior. Offerings to him consist of a farmer's food, viz. *bajra roti* and stuffed brinjal. To meet this God of the commons, to hail him with Yelkot and to immerse oneself in the holy turmeric falling all around, you have to come to Jejuri. Jejuri stands 40 km from Pune, on the Saaswad route.

JEJURI

7. Bhuleshwar

I had been hearing about the Bhuleshwar temple near Yavat on the Pune-Solapur road, for quite some time from my friend Nitin Abhyankar. He owns a farm-house near Yavat and hence keeps going there often. He told me of an amusing occurrence in this temple. The priest keeps 5 *pedhas* (a kind of sweet) offered by devotees, in a small bowl and places the bowl in a small groove in front of the main Shivlinga there. The Shivlinga has a brass mask that can be moved back and forth such that the niche in front of it is covered. When the bowl with *pedhas* is placed inside the niche, one *pedha* disappears in the next 3-4 minutes! On hearing about this miracle, I was immensely curious to see it for myself and thus set out for Bhuleshwar, armed with my Handycam!

Around 42 km from Pune, on the Pune-Solapur road, is the Bhuleshwar bypass. Three kilometres from the entrance of this bypass, is the Yavat village. Fifteen kilometres from here, is a scenic spot called Narayanbet. Tourists go to Narayanbet for bird-watching. Seven kilometres towards the right of Bhuleshwar bypass is a hillock on which stands the Bhuleshwar temple. Ninad Bedekar narrated a short history of this place: In 1629, Murar Jagdev razed the fort of Pune with a plough driven by donkeys and relocated Pune's police-station to Bhuleshwar. At the lower end of the temple is the bastion with a protective wall around it. The surrounding area has been bestowed the name Daulat Manglai, due to the presence at the southern side of the temple. A 3-4 m-long ledge has been erected in this area. A 13th-century Ganesha idol, in the garb of a woman and in the sitting position, belonging to the Yadav era, can be seen here. It is addressed as Lambodari, Ganeshwari or Ganeshyani.

Apart from the miraculous events experienced here, the temple is also worth seeing for its beautiful architecture and intricate carving. On its walls and ceilings, are sculptures of elephants and tigers, reminding you of the Kopeshwar temple of Khidrapur. We went inside the temple and asked to see the Shivlinga and the niche. I personally checked the niche to see if it contained any burrow or smaller niche for rodents to come in. But the niche, carved in stone, had absolutely no such opening. After thorough inspection, I asked the priest to place the bowl of *pedhas*, even as I video-filmed the entire thing. He kept the bowl inside and shifted the mask to cover it. We peeked inside after 3-4 minutes and to my utter dismay, all the 5 *pedhas* were intact! I then asked the priest if the disappearance was connected in any way to the concepts of *paap-punya* (good and bad deeds) of the person who kept the *pedhas*. To my further dismay,

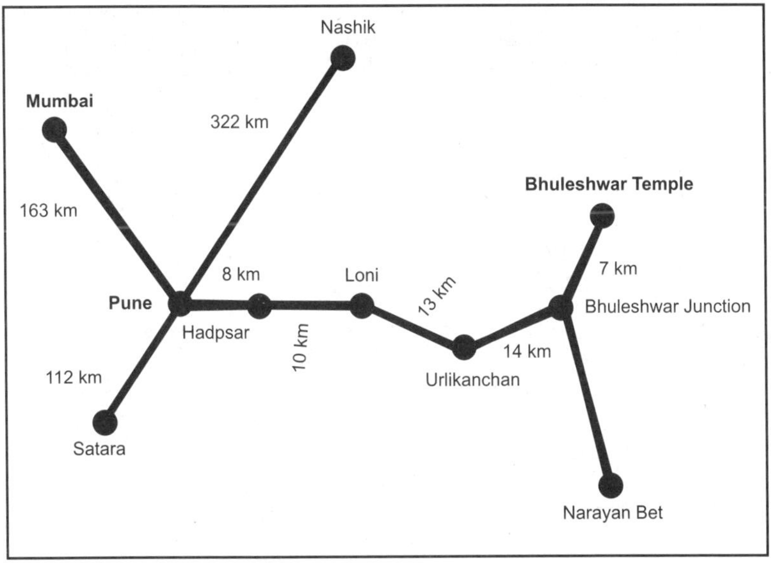

Bhuleshwar Temple

THE PLACE WHERE THE *PEDHAS* ARE PLACED

he replied in the affirmative. But, I decided to again place 5 *pedhas*. After doing so, when the mask was again shifted to reveal the *pedhas* after a few minutes, I was overjoyed to find one *pedha* missing! Quite a few devotees came in after that, including a Sikh family. They all placed the *pedhas* and each time one *pedha* was found missing. It was actually miraculous to see the *pedha* go missing! There was no chance of any rodent coming here; even if it had, there would have been some noise created, but there was none. Even the priest was sitting at some distance. It was surreal. It is imperative to explore the scientific rationale behind this amazing phenomenon. None of the people I talked to – be it the priest, villagers, other devotees etc – could give me any logical explanation for this. They simply vouched for the fact that it has been happening for years now!

I had seen a similar kind of miracle at the Kamarali Durvesh shrine near Shivapur on the Pune-Satara road. Eleven people had lifted a 100-kg boulder on their fingers! Similarly, I had seen a heavy-built man entering via a 1 sq.ft entrance into the shrine of a Nathpanthiya saint, near Saaswad.

People had given at least one scientific reason behind these phenomena. It is thus essential that someone unearth the science behind the occurrence at Bhuleshwar too.

Anyway, either to experience this miracle or to simply visit this beautiful, holy place, one must come to Bhuleshwar.

From Bhuleshwar, the road goes ahead to Saaswad. Purandar fort lies on the way. One can visit the temple during daytime, experience the sunset at Purandar and return to Pune at night.

8. Akkalkot

Amongst the many pirs and saints of Maharashtra, most devotees are well aware of the three famous ones, viz. Gajanan Maharaj of Shegaon, Saibaba of Shirdi and Swami Samarth of Akkalkot. A one-time place of residence of Swami Samarth, Akkalkot comes in the Solapur district. Situated a few kilometres off the Solapur-Hyderabad road, this 400-year-old shrine has become a very important religious place in Maharashtra today.

As with any other religious place, the shops near the temple sell lockets, keychains etc with Swami's picture on it. There are also many ships selling puja paraphernalia such as flowers, *thaalis*, incense sticks etc. There are 2-3 places in Akkalkot, where Swami had stayed. Amongst those, the Vatvruksha Swami Maharaj Mandir has been constructed by the then-king of Akkalkot and a big devotee of Swami Samartha, Maloji Raje. One enters a sprawling courtyard on stepping inside this temple. An enormous banyan tree standing right in the centre of the courtyard, attracts your attention. One feels a unique sense of calm on sitting in the shade of this banyan tree. There's a ritual of first paying respects to the Shivalinga installed in a small temple near Swami's temple and then go into Swami's temple to pay obeisance.

Akkalkot Temple Sanctum

When I reached Swami's temple, the *aarti* was going on. I was fortunate enough to take part in the *aarti* for which there were throngs of people inside and outside the temple.

Near the temple, are Swami's private quarters. There's a huge photograph of Swami kept in these quarters. This picture was clicked by a photographer from Kodak Company and there's an amusing story related to the same. When the photographer first clicked Swami's picture without taking his permission, he got a blank plate when he developed the picture! Then, he got permission to click Swami after making special requests. However, after he developed this set of photos, he could see different Gods at different times in it and yet, not a single picture showed Swami! He got very depressed and finally begged Swami to let him click his picture. Finally Swami relented; the photographer got his picture and it is this picture which is the only authentic one available of Swami today! There's a small temple-like structure outside the main temple. It is said, that if you insert your head in this structure and place your ear to the ground, you can hear the beats of a mridangam. There's a well in front of the temple. It is said, that earlier this well had salty water. When Swami came to Akkalkot and asked for water from this well, it turned sweet! Even today, the cool, sweet water of the well placates your body and soul like nothing else!

There's a *bhojnalay* (hotel-cum-catering service) run by the temple's trust. The food prepared here is first offered to Swami amidst sacred chants and then the devotees are given the same food, free of cost. It is called Mahaprasad. Hundreds of people eat the Mahaprasad daily. The hotel has a picture of Swami and an eight-armed idol of Goddess Durga. After placing the offering in front of Swami, an *aarti* is done here. I was fortunate to partake of this *aarti* too.

In the temple's surroundings, is a huge idol of Swami. The scholarly pandit of Maidergir, Madhavshastri, has written an ode to Swami's

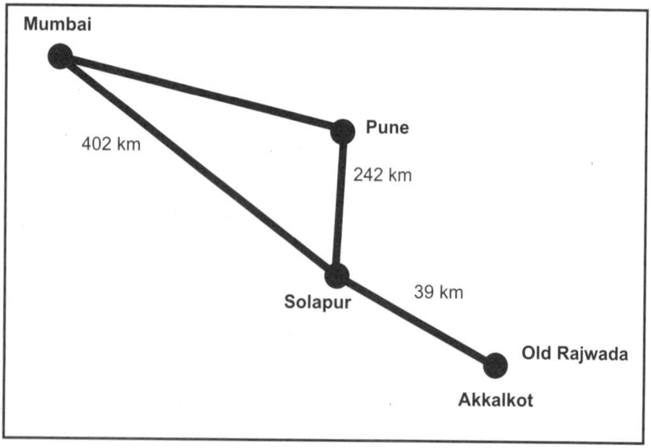

appearance in Sanskrit, after he saw Swami for the first time. He has written that standing at 6½ ft, Swami was glowing akin to the Sun-God. His feet were dainty as a lotus and there was a golden aura surrounding his face.

Vatvruksha Mandir Vishwast Samiti has erected a bhaktaniwas (lodge for devotees) on Gangapur road. Over 1000 devotees can stay here at a time. There's also a good hotel in the premises of the lodge. Soon, the trust intends to open a hospital and an old age home.

Rajerai math

Near the main temple is the Rajerai Math (shrine). Shankarrao Rajerai was the jagirdar (feudal lord) of Hyderabad territory. He was severely afflicted by tuberculosis. All doctors, hakims failed to provide him respite from the disease. Finally, he came to Gangapur in search of a cure. A miraculous revelation led him to Akkalkot, where he promised to donate Rs 10,000 if cured of the disease. Swami cured him and he donated Rs 10,000 at Swami's feet. But Swami refused to touch the money; insisting that he instead make a shrine near the temple of Shri Ram over here.

Swami proclaimed "this will be my retreat!" Thus came up the Rajerai math.

The panchdhaatu (five metal mix) idol of Swami seen in the math, was installed on 6th December 1996 on the eve of Champashashthi. However the padukas (clogs) here are very old. In the Magh month of 1877, Swami himself had got the clogs for his feet created and installed here with his very hands.

The beautiful eight-armed idol of Durga Devi seen here was made in 1964 by Shivaji Gajul. Since 1953, Belenath Maharaj has been residing in the math. One experiences a divine sense of calm and quietude in this 124-year-old math. Swami, while entering the math, used to easily touch the overhead arch of the 7 ft tall doorway. One can imagine the stature of the *ajanubahu* Swami (one whose arms reach to the knees) from this itself!

9. Akkalkot's Old and New Palaces

Most people know Akkalkot as the place of origin of Swami Samartha Maharaj. But few know that Akkalkot was also the capital city of the royal family of the Raje-Bhosales. Even today, while seeing the frontal part of the palace, one gets awed by the strong protective wall around the palace. The intricately carved pillars (to light lamps) are also standing strong, to date.

However, most of the stone construction has collapsed now. Wild shrubs and grass have taken over most of the palace. However, with proper and carefully done renovation and restoration, the palace can still stand tall - as in yesteryears.

There are statues sculpted in stone standing around the palace; but they're in ruins now. I also saw a stone tablet with inscriptions in some South Indian language but couldn't decipher what was written on it.

Some distance away from the palace is the royal graveyard. The arched construction seen here, is the grave of Fattesingh Maharaj. One can also see a huge banyan tree here; its circumference is indeed awe-inspiringly large!

One can see a lot of small and big cannons lined up in front of the new palace. Three of these cannons were also used in the Second World War. A stone tablet with the snake-god and other gods carved on it is found here, along with an idol of Lord Shiva with a dumroo in hand.

In the palace's verandah, a stuffed leopard, killed during one of the hunting excursions, has been placed. Though one knows that it is a dead animal, the leopard's aggressive stance and glinting eyes send a chill down the spine.

There's an armoury (weapon-house) on the first storey of the palace. Its first room comprises mainly of swords. The varied shapes and sizes of these swords make for interesting viewing. One can also see formidable cast-iron armours over here.

There are also a lot of guns to be seen here. Many of these were gifted to Fattesingh Maharaj by his British official friends. But the officials were quite cunning. They gifted him the guns only after making them useless for firing! But the length of these guns is worth seeing. Such huge guns are rarely seen nowadays. These long guns were used to scare people/enemies at the foothills of the palace.

The local guide told me quite a bit of history about this armoury and the weapons therein. We all have seen a 'sinhasan' (a lion's seat or throne) but the throne in this palace is a 'gajasan' (a throne with an elephant's legs). It seems that the expectation behind such a throne was that its occupant, apart from being strong, intelligent and courageous like an elephant, should also be able to lead his followers successfully.

There's a photograph of Fattesingh Maharaj in the armoury. He deserves special mention for creating such a fabulous compilation of arms in his short life of 28 years!

'Satyamev Jayate' was the slogan of the Raje-Bhosales. It is today found on the national emblem as well! Today the palace and the museum are looked after by Sunita Raje and Sanyukta Raje, the heirs of the family.

Finally Swami relented; the photographer got his picture and it is this picture which is the only authentic one available of Swami today!

One can see a variety of headgears; apart from various vessels, utensils, plates etc. The horns, skins etc of animals hunted down by Fattesingh Maharaj are also seen. There's a huge ostrich egg to be seen here. It is as big as a coconut! On coming to Akkalkot, apart from visiting Swami's shrine, one must also visit this museum.

The distance between Solapur and Akkalkot is 35 km and there are many buses plying daily between the two places.

The ST bus charge for one person from various places is as follows:

Pune to Akkalkot – Rs 240
Mumbai to Akkalkot – Rs 440
Nagpur to Akkalkot – Rs 740

Food and accommodation: One can get excellent free meals at the dining hall/hotel of Swami's shrine. Apart from that, the village has many good hotels. You can stay at the Bhaktaniwas, the Rajerai math or at the small lodges in the village.

10. Tuljapur

There are many manifestations of the Aadimaya (Goddess Ambabai). Not only is she a manifestation of the surrounding nature, she is also the slayer of all evils. There are many difficult modes of penance to please the Goddess. Similar rituals are practised in front of the Goddess of Tuljapur (Tuljapur Bhawani). Jogtinis (female devotees), under the influence of the Devi, let their hair free and keep rotating to the loud beats of instruments – reminding one of the terrifying form of Goddess Durga.

The main hall of the temple has sixteen pillars made of stone; as is usually seen in Hemadpanti temples. Even the pillars in this temple are intricately carved. Besides this hall, is a small hall standing on three pillars.

During amavasya (no-moon day), purnima (full-moon day), navratra and other festivals, the temple is filled to the brim with devotees, especially jogtinis. They sing songs in the praise of the Goddess, in a high pitch, in keeping with numerous instruments. It is a privilege of the jogtinis to sing these songs. The sanctum sanctorum stands just beside the main hall. In the sanctum sanctorum is a beautiful silver eight-armed idol of Goddess Tuljabhawani.

When I went into the temple, I experienced a divine serenity and immense contentment on seeing the idol of Goddess Tuljabhawani. The goddess is the family deity of not only the great Shiv Chhatrapati, the establisher of Hindavi Swaraj; but of almost the entire Maharashtra. I conducted the puja of the Goddess; which was followed by the aarti, in praise of this slayer of evils.

Now, the idol is adorned by ornaments and clothes but the original idol is also very beautiful. Above the 3 feet high, eight-armed idol of the Goddess is the 'sa-yoni

Wish-fulfilling stone of Chintamani

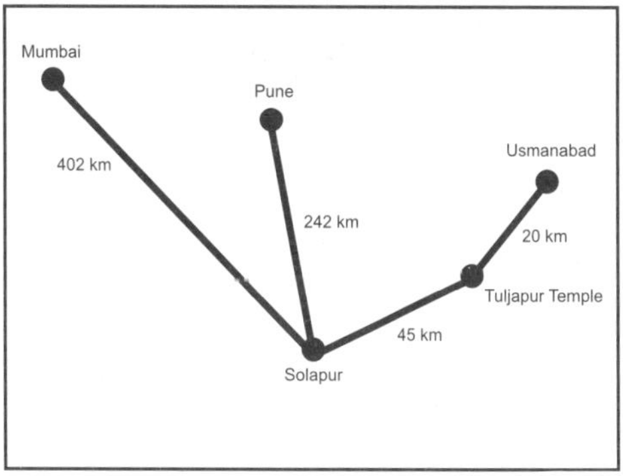

linga'. The sun and moon are carved on the either sides of the Goddess who is shown towering over the demon Mahishasura.

'Tulja' is a manifestation of Goddess Bhawani. It must have developed from the Sanskrit name Turja or Tvarja. Tuljabhawani is also called as Tukai. Tukka and Shukra (in the Dravidian language) i.e. Friday is an important day for paying obeisance to this Goddess. Hence she is also known as Tukai i.e. the Goddess of Friday!

Goddess Tuljabhawani is prayed to in various ways, in Maharashtra. The male devotees are called Jogtas and the female ones are called Jogtinis. One can always see jogtinis wearing a necklace of conch-shells; green glass bangles adorning their hands; red vermillion smeared on their foreheads, roaming around with a basket containing the Goddess's mask, on their heads. They collect food by invoking the Goddess's name saying *Tuljabhawanicha ude ude* and live on the alms thus collected. Just as we have the waghya-murli at Jejuri, so do we have the jogtas-jogtinis at Tuljapur.

Behind the main temple, is the unique Chintamani dagad (wish granting stone). If one's wish is going to be fulfilled, the stone rotates to the right, when you place your palms on it, and if not, it goes left! I hesitantly placed my palms on the stone and asked for three wishes. I was thrilled to see that the stone turned right all the three times!

Every Marathi *manoos* comes at least once in a lifetime to pay a visit to this slayer of evils and creator of good!

Although Tuljapur is geographically located in the Dharashir district, it is quite close to Solapur, 45 km only! Dharashiv to Tuljapur is 23 km.

The ST bus fare for one person is as follows:

Pune to Tuljapur – Rs 220
Mumbai to Tuljapur – Rs 440
Nagpur to Tuljapur – Rs 720

Lodging and food – Tuljapur is a taluka and devotees from all over Maharashtra as also the neighbouring Karnataka and Andhra Pradesh flock here. Thus there are good hotels to accommodate all of them. There are some dormitories in the village. If informed in advance, accommodation can also be arranged at villagers' houses. Otherwise, there are great hotels available at Solapur.

11. Naldurg Fort

The fort's history: Naldurg is located in the Tuljapur taluka of Osmanabad district. There's not much history documented about the Naldurg fort. It is speculated to have been built in AD 1561 during the reign of Ali Adilshah. Since the main routes to Paranda Solapur, Vijapur etc used to go from Naldurg, this place had acquired immense importance in the days of yore. This unique and historically important fort is divided into four main parts from within viz. Ramdurg, Shahadurg, Ranamandal and the main fort.

The fort's geographical position: Naldurg is a semi-rural place in the Marathwada district and its strong and formidable fort adds to the scenic beauty of the place. The fort is 47 km away from Tuljapur and 45 km to the east of Solapur. The fort encompasses the surrounding 5-7 km (in terms of radius) and is naturally located on the banks of a river that flows right through the middle of the fort!

The type of fort: Naldurg is a flatland fort with a circumference of 1½ miles! Bastions are built on all three sides of the fort.

The fort's walls: The fort's walls are made of strong stone and are thus extremely formidable.

The fort's bastions: There are many bastions on this fort; with the main one being 'Upali buruj' (Upali bastion). It is the tallest and biggest bastion here. The bastion stands tall at a height of 125 ft and has seventy steps. At the top, is a huge cannon. It must have been used to strike the enemy dead with a torrent of cannon-balls, during war-time. There's a beautiful palace and an ammunition-warehouse on this bastion. Apart from this, the Paranda buruj, Naagin buruj made in the wall, Sangram buruj containing an elephant-shaped cannon made of five metals, Bandanwaj buruj etc present on the fort give a clear idea of the high security measures adopted on it.

The fort's entrance: There are seven doorways in the fort. The main entrance is called Hubegul. It is a wooden door with intricately carved wooden nets fitted onto it to provide protection during a fire attack by the enemy! This door has huge iron nails fitted onto it, so as to not crumble against an elephant's attack! The other doorways are Hazaarshetty darwaza, Panimahal darwaza, Ramnaar darwaza, Hatti darwaza and Panthaat darwaza.

Various constructions on the Naldurg fort:

1) Rajwada: There's a palace on the fort. It is in shambles now but the ruins point towards a formerly grand building.

2) Jama masjid: Just a few feet away from the main entrance is the Jama masjid (mosque) built by Ibrahim Adilshah.

3) Baaradari: This construction is close to the protective wall and one can get a beautiful view of the river and its dam from here. This building, divided into two parts and situated on a turn of the Bori River, is an example of great architecture.

4) Machhli tat: The Bori River flows from outside the fort on the fort's eastern side. This bank is called as Machhli tat. This is a scenic location because from here, the river cascades over huge boulders. The scene gets further enhanced during monsoons.

5) Ranamandal and Parkot: Ranamandal or Chhota killa as it was called, was most probably a war-camp and was used to train soldiers.

6) Paani Mahal: There's a beautiful building on the fort called Paani Mahal. From an inscription on a tablet found here, it is assumed that this was built in the reign of Adilshah. This is the most scenic spot in the whole fort. During monsoons, when the river gets flooded, it cascades from above, with the sunlight intermingling in it to form a beautiful rainbow. A glance at the far end of the river shows some beautiful scenery. Ibrahim Adilshah manoeuvred the river mid-way into the fort and constructed a dam over it to ensure a steady supply of water to the fort. The palace is decorated with intricate carving and the view outside it is a breathtaking one. Especially, the beauty to the north of the fort, which can be seen through the huge windows and arches of the palace, is mesmerising. The Paani Mahal is approximately

PAANI MAHAL AT NALDURG

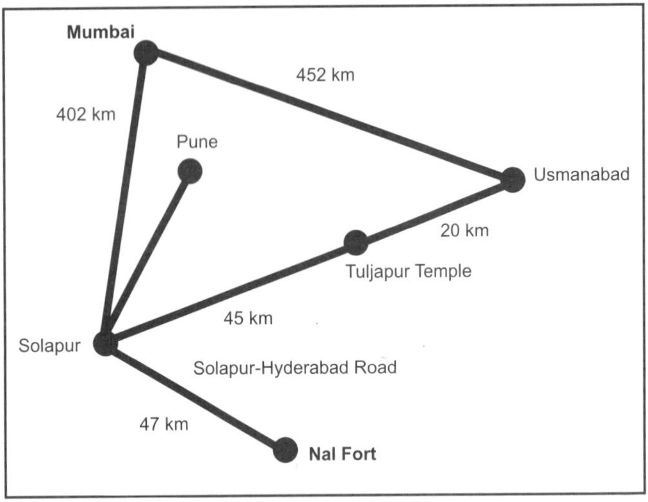

100 ft long. Its construction is such that it'll pose a challenge to modern engineers wanting to unravel the techniques behind it. The Farsi-inscribed tablet found here proves that this building was built in AD 1022 in the reign of Sultan Ibrahim Adilshah II, which was also a very golden period, in terms of the fortunes of this fort. Next to this palace is a flour mill that runs with the help of water-turbines.

7) Rani Mahal: Today this palace is in utter ruins but once upon a time it was supposed to be famous for its excellent carving.

8) A fort protected from all sides: With ravines to the west and south of the fort and a river to its east and north, the fort is well-protected from all sides. In fact, at the east, the river meanders from near a steep slope (precipice) and thus provides a fabulous protection from enemies. The river has been cleverly used to enhance the fort's security.

Today, even though this area is considered as a rural one, in the past it was a very wealthy, glorious town. The Chalukya, Bahamani, Adilshahi etc fiefdoms had their reign on this fort. From the perspective of warfare, this fort was considered unconquerable.

Crossing over the wall of this fort, we come to its adjacent fort. The protective wall of this fort is also very strong. This fort, in all probability, must be used as an alternative security measure.

There's a regular bus-service from 45 km east of Solapur on the Solapur-Hyderabad highway; as well as 47 km from Tuljapur to come to Naldurg. There's great arrangement for food, near Naldurg itself.

12. Solapur's Siddharameshwar Temple

The famous Siddharameshwar mandir (temple), lake and the wall of one fort are all very scenic spots of Solapur. The temple is quite huge. Very rarely seen cleanliness is experienced here! There are shops selling holy paraphernalia in the temple's courtyard. The scenic surroundings and the beautiful architecture of the temple have made it a pride of Solapur. There's a strong stony protective wall around the temple. When we arrived here, preparations were going on for a festival wherein the temple is lit up with 1 lakh lights!

The temple has been built in stone and is kept extremely spick and span. The 68 Shivlingas installed by Siddharameshwar are found here. There's also a small Ganesh temple. After paying respects to Lord Ganesh, I came to the main temple. Carefully tended trees add to the beauty of the temple. The cleanliness and beauty of the temple make it a very holy experience to be here. The Samadhi of Siddharameshwar is situated at the centre of the temple. There's also an idol of only Vitthal (sans Rakhumai), akin to the one at Pandharpur – made in black stone and with hands on the hips.

From the newly-designed hall, I came into the old one. After crossing this small structure balanced on stone pillars, we come to the sanctum sanctorum. There's a Shivlinga with a mask made of gold over here. In front of it is a nandi (bull) made of silver.

Coming out of the temple, one sees a huge lake. Solapur is generally a drought-prone area. But surprisingly, the water from this lake never dries up! Not even when there's no water in the entire Solapur! The temple gets added beauty due to the lake. It's a joyful experience to travel the entire lake in a boat.

Anyone will be prompted to capture the beauty of this lake; as was evident looking at two schoolgirls painting the lake onto their drawing papers!

The temple, lit up in 1 lakh lights looked marvellous during night-time. Known as the gateway of South Maharashtra, Solapur is convenient to reach via rail or road. There's a recently- introduced Intercity Express from Pune to Solapur (225 km).

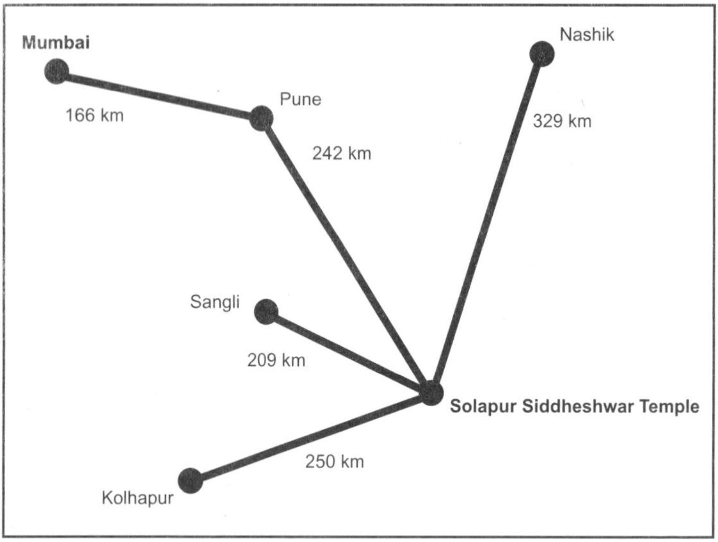

Distance:

Pune to Solapur – 225 km

Mumbai to Solapur – 345 km

Fares for one person by ST bus:

Pune to Solapur – Rs 220; Mumbai to Solapur – Rs 440; Nagpur to Solapur – Rs 780

But surprisingly, the water from this lake never dries up! Not even when there's no water in the entire Solapur!

Lodging and food: There are many good hotels in Solapur which is a big city. You can choose from small hotels to three-starred ones! Rates vary from Rs 200 to Rs 1500. The food available is also excellent.

13. Marathwada

The musical stones of Deglur near Nanded

Sometimes you don't know what awaits you when you are travelling. I have explored most of Maharashtra but a portion of Eastern Maharashtra better known as Marathwada was yet to be tapped. It so happened that I was invited for the inauguration of a cultural music programme called Aashadhotsav by a Shivsena zilla-pramukh (district-head) Mr Hemant Patil. It was a great programme with stalwarts like Arun Date and Hridaynath Mangeshkar performing. After the inauguration I had a full day left before catching a return flight back to Mumbai and I generally utilize such time for exploring and investigating new and interesting places close by. While talking to Hemant's colleagues Mr Sanjay Undavat, a local nature lover Shailendra and photographer Mr Aundhkar I got the information that there was a fabulous fort of Kandhar around 51 km from Nanded; Sachkhand Saheb Gurudwara in Nanded city, a great stone temple at Hottal and a dargah at Deglur about 85 km from Nanded on the Maharashtra-Andhra Pradesh border. Both the dargah and the temple have stone structures which when hit by a smaller stone piece in hand, produce seven specific notes of Hindustani classical music sa,re,ga,ma,pa,dha,ni. There were locals who believed that such a stone was also in Kandhar fort so we decided to visit the fort first. Kandhar is a bhumikot killa or a fort built on flat land. It was built during the reign of the Rashtrakut dynasty. Kakatiya rulers Prataprudra and Somdeo constructed the fort. The walls of this fort are 120 ft high and are surrounded by 100 ft wide ditch all around. The fort is spread over 20 acres of land and has 34 bastions. It was conquered in 1327 AD by Mallik Ambar. Then, Hasan Gangu Bahamani also controlled the fort for some time. Thus later, it was in hands of Nizamshahi, Baridshahi and also Mughalshahi. Ambari buruj or Ambari bastion retains the memory of Malik Ambar. It is in a dilapidated condition now and was recently given support by cementing the walls which doesn't go with the original black stone structure. In its heyday, the fort has seen beautiful gardens water tanks and water fountains. The garden inside was called Rashk-e-Kashmir as mentioned in the Persian inscription in the fort and was thus compared with the beauty of Kashmir. The fort has other important structures inside like Haji Sayyad Saidufin Rafai dargah, a barudkhana where ammunition used to be stored, and the hamamkhana or public bathroom. On the Ambari buruj one can see a huge Ambari cannon whose frontal part resembles a tiger's face. But the most interesting is the sculpture of a yaksha called Khetrapal Bharav which is kept in pieces inside the fort. It is 62 feet high and 0.62 metre wide with a huge face. Its 1.7 metre long feet are particularly noteworthy. It was a very fruitful visit to this fort though I was a little disappointed to not have found the musical stone. Later after confirming with many people we started off for Deglur and Hottal to see the dargah and temple having these stones.

We moved towards Deglur which is very close to Andhra Pradesh-Maharashtra border. After reaching Deglur it would have been difficult to find that particular dargah had not Mr. Aundhkar, a person who had seen it before, accompanied us. It is a very small unassuming place off the main road. Luckily the caretaker was inside. He showed us the dargah from within, giving brief information about it. It is a dargah of a pir named Sayyad Ziyauddin Rafael Kadri. The main tomb is in the basement. Then he took us outside and there were those stones placed equidistant in straight line. He took a small stone in his hand for demonstration and started banging the stone in his hand over the top of each square piece of stone one after the other. One could hear a distinct change in notes. A person used to listening to classical music can easily identify the notes as sa,re,ga,ma,pa,dha,ni,sa. He continued hitting at faster rate actually running and we could hear proper music. It was a fascinating experience. It seems the stones are specially carved and kept hollow with varying densities that's why when struck with another stone they produce musical notes. One can't but admire the skills of sculptors of those days who had not more than a hammer and chisel at their disposal to do such a magnificent job. From Deglur, Hottal is approx 12 km on Nanded-Bidar road. All heritage sites are at a walkable distance in the village. One can call this a Chalukyan temple town.

PLAYING THE MUSICAL STONES

The 3 temples in Hottal are

great art-creations displaying the same majestic heritage of Ajanta and Ellora caves that are found near Aurangabad. Out of these the Siddheshwar temple in Hottal was built by Siddhugi, a subordinate ruler from Chalukyan dynasty. It consists of a mukhamandapa, mandapa, two ardhmandapas, antarala and garbhgriha. In the mukhamandapa, which is erected on a massive square; 16 huge, beautifully-decorated pillars stand supporting the roof. The first floor of mandapa has a circular flower carved out of stone. The temple stands on 4 ft high plinth. On the exterior walls are exotic figures of gods and goddesses like Ganesh, Kali, Shiva, Nataraja etc.

Just behind Siddheshwar is the Mahadev temple, which is now dismantled for renovation. The locals showed us one long carved piece of stone saying that it produces musical notes. We tried in the same way as in Deglur dargah. The stone here was in one piece and produced different notes at different lengths; but not as distinctly as in Deglur. The third temple of Someshwar is in the east of Hottal. It is similar in construction but has an inscription on stone giving lot of info about the Chalukyan era. Among few other things worth a visit in and around Nanded are the Sachkhand Saheb Gurudwara in the city and a mosque known as the Hazrat Nawab Sarfaraz Khan Sahid masjid at Biloli situated 70 km from Nanded. Hazrat Khan was earlier employed in Aurangzeb's army. The mosque was constructed 330 years back. It has 4 minarets – the one on the north has 8 chains.

Another beautiful temple 60 km east of Nanded is the Narsimha Mandir on the southern banks of Godavari River. There's also a Maa Saraswati temple at Basar on Maharashtra-Andhra border, 52 km from Nanded. It is worth a dekko as the only Saraswati Mandir in the state. People take their children there to pay obeisance before beginning their education as Saraswati is considered the goddess of education.

14. Enigmatic Phenomena

In this book, there have been many such places listed wherein one can experience natural or divine phenomena. Many people have experienced these; some have also been experienced by me personally. Some have been recorded for documentation.

I'm often asked whether I have ever experienced ghosts or some such supernatural beings whilst touring across dense forests, eerie mountains and faraway villages. I can't say for sure whether they have been ghosts but at times, I've felt something unusual around myself. Till I am fully convinced, I can't say that they were ghosts!

The most memorable experience on these lines was at Mhaismaal. This is a not-so-renowned place, with a cool weather. The mountain at Aurangabad, in whose belly the Ellora caves are located, has Mhaismaal at its peak. It is not too high from ground-level but since the area around is sparse, one can see till afar from this place. Strong winds blowing in the face, a cool atmosphere and millions of lights glowing in the valley below, make it a favourite pastime of mine to sit outside the government rest-house at night. This rest-house is located at the very edge of the precipice. In the past, I've taken my bike or jeep and stayed there alone as well.

I recently went there again with two friends. A friend had some work at a factory in Aurangabad. We decided to come to Mhaismaal after his work was over. We reached at night, in his Fiat. It was almost 11-11.30 pm when we went to bed after a meal, and a hearty chat-session. We had to wake up early in the morning. Since there was a power-cut and it was getting steamy in the room, we slept in the verandah outside the room. We placed our beds at some distance from each

Saibaba

other and promptly went off to sleep. Around midnight, I felt someone shaking me vigorously out of sleep. I immediately awoke. My friends were deep in slumber. There was no one to be seen around. I thought I had seen a bad dream and decided against waking up my friends. I went back to sleep, and soon, I again felt someone shaking me vigorously. This time, I got frightened and also alert! This was certainly not a dream. I finally awoke my friends; they did not believe me but nevertheless, all of us stayed awake the rest of the night. Of course, due to lack of evidence I haven't related this story to many people.

Similar experiences have been had by the veteran traveller-writer GoNiDa aka G. N. Dandekar. He has narrated these experiences in his wonderful travelogue 'Durgbhramangatha'. Towards the end of Rajmachi fort, where one has to cross the Ulhas river waterfall, GoNiDa felt someone walking alongside him. Since he was alone, he ran towards the waterfall; safe in the knowledge that ghosts fear water. GoNiDa cupped his hands to drink water and....to his utter bewilderment he saw another pair of cupped hands drinking water right beside him! No wonder, he ran for dear life from there.

Many people have also mentioned having a similar experience on Torna fort. There's a stone belonging to the spirit of a Brahman called Diwekar, on Torna fort. The offerings made to this stone have been sponsored by the Maharashtra Government! Author P.K Ghanekar has mentioned in his book "Saad Sahyadrichi, Bhatkanti Killyanchi" about people sighting someone waving a red lantern from the Srimangai temple on Torna fort.

Sixteen kilometres from Bhandardara, near the foothills of Kalsubai, is a small village called Khed-Bhairav. I had gone there for shooting. The villagers tell a tale, akin to ones read in Jim Corbett's books, about the Bhairoba temple situated there. The temple is deserted during the night.

During Navratra, each day a tiger comes to visit the temple – or so the villagers say. But of course, otherwise too, tigers roam freely in the area. In fact, there's also a small temple devoted to the tiger over here!

Well, the truth about these phenomena is yet to be unearthed completely; but such stories abound in plenty in the valleys of Maharashtra and it is indeed fun listening to them! Apart from these eerie and somewhat scary experiences, I've also been fortunate to encounter some divine supernatural phenomena in the course of my travels. Maharashtra is a land blessed by the presence of many peers and saints. Amongst them the three main saints are Swami Samartha Maharaj, Shri Gajanan Maharaj and Shri Saibaba.

I got a chance to conduct thorough research about Shri Saibaba (of whom I'm also a keen devotee) thanks to my profession as an actor. It so happened that a film producer from London, who is also an ardent devotee of Lord Sai and wanted to make a movie on him, during his search for an actor in the title role, repeatedly visualized me in the same. He had seen a couple of movies of mine but did not know anything more about me – not even my name. But something prompted him to come to India and enquire about me. So sure was he of finding and casting me that he erected a set worth lakhs of rupees even before he contacted me through director Mithu Singh. His enquiries led him to discover that I was famed for my negative portrayals in many Bollywood movies! But neither this information nor advice from his acquaintances against casting me in the title role could change his mind and I am now portraying Lord Saibaba in the ambitious, big-budget movie that he is making!

Once cast, I became immensely interested in unearthing information about Saibaba. Actually, devotion to Lord Sai remains firmly entrenched in our family for years now. My great-grandfather Shri Nagesh Vasudeo Gunaji had translated into English, the Sai-Charitra (biography of Lord Sai) belonging to the Sai Sansthan of Shirdi and written by Shri Dabholkar. More than one lakh copies of this translated version have been sold worldwide till date. Thus, I have had immense experiences of Lord Sai and the role evoked further interest in me to research about this great saint.

SAIBABA PLAYS HIDE-AND-SEEK!

My search led me to Shri Shrirang Nulkar of Satara whose great-grandfather was a very close acquaintance and devotee of Lord Sai. Sai used to fondly address him as *mhatara* (old man) – so close was their bond. Shrirang Nulkar's parents graciously invited me to their home and gave me invaluable information about Sai's mannerisms, nature, his Vaidarbhiya Marathi dialect, instances that occurred in his connection etc. Shrirang also showed me a rare photo of Saibaba and narrated an interesting incident behind it saying, "This photograph was shot when Saibaba was on his way to Lendibaug with some acquaintances. The photographer initially clicked the photo without taking Saibaba's permission and thus, when developed, all the other things were clearly visible except for Saibaba himself, who chose to hide behind a veneer of mist (or so it seems) with just his feet visible! Only when the photographer asked for forgiveness followed by permission, did the picture get snapped properly!"

Shrirang further directed me to his younger brother Sudhanshu Nulkar, who stays at Kurla in Mumbai. Meeting Sudhanshu proved to be an even more blessed occurrence; for, he showed me some amazing and rare things from his personal treasure, which belonged to Lord Sai. Amongst them was a *kafni* (cloth) belonging to Lord Sai which smells distinctly of sandalwood even today, almost hundred years later; a mala (beaded necklace) and a few ancient coins given by Lord Sai to the Nulkars. I was indeed very lucky to see the rare photograph and these other things that hardly anybody gets to see!

Towards the end of Rajmachi fort, where one has to cross the Ulhas river waterfall, GoNiDa felt someone walking alongside him.

GOA

1. A Unique Rendezvous

Here I am recounting a tour of unique traveller-oriented locales in the region spread across Goa and Karnataka, belonging to the Kadamb family.

Some coincidences are indeed unique and I experienced one such at a function where I met Mr Bhushan Kadamb, a direct descendant of the royal Kadamb family. This meeting led to me visiting (with him) a number of interesting places owned by this illustrious family. The opportunity was also cherished for the fact that since these are privately-owned places, I wouldn't have been able to see them otherwise, had I not met Bhushan.

As such, I have encountered very many known-unknown destinations across Maharashtra and I have also tried to portray them as well as possible via my books and the TV programme *Bhatkanti*. As it is I'm fond of scouring new places; thus, when I come across such new and interesting places, I like to research thoroughly about the same and present it before an avid audience. That's because everyone is curious to know more about unexplored, enigmatic places and phenomena.

In the interim, there was a small function hosted by the Mohite Patils on behalf of the Maharashtra Tourism Development Corporation (MTDC) when they were handling the same. While speaking to Bhushan during this function, I realized that he is well-acquainted with many Bollywood stars. Sunil Shetty and Sanjay Dutt are his especially close buddies. But I was even more pleasantly surprised to know that

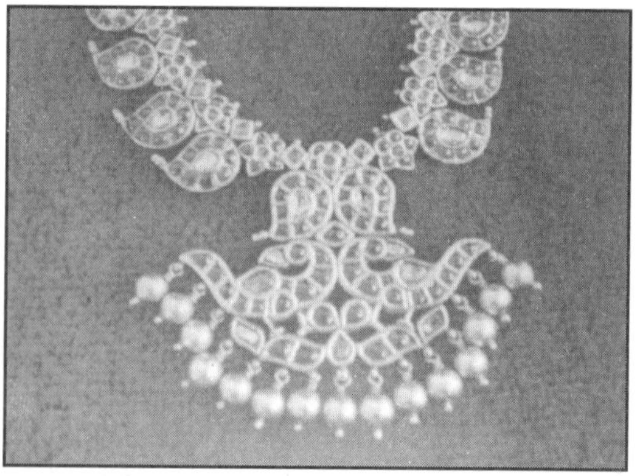

A BEAUTIFUL ANTIQUE NECKLACE, A FAMILY HEIRLOOM

he and his brother Atul Kadamb have read all my books and are well-versed in Maharashtra's history and tourism.

I came especially close to the Kadambs due to three reasons: one, my mother also hails from Goa; secondly, both brothers take deep interest in Marathi literature and poetry and thirdly, they, like me, have deepest reverence and devotion to Chhatrapati Shivaji Maharaj.

In our first meeting itself, the Kadambs invited me to Goa. What's more, they also insisted on taking me on a tour of all the forts, places etc in the areas of Goa and Karnataka where they reigned. Till then, I had only read or heard about the royal families like Chalukya, Rashatrakut, Shilahar, Kadamb, Satvahan etc; but to associate with an heir (albeit dressed in civil attire) of one of those families was no less than a treat for me!

Without wasting more time, we decided on a mutually convenient date and off I set for Goa! Generally, I'm never fussy about the mode of transport while travelling; jeeps, ST buses, motorbikes – anything goes! Of course, if a comfortable vehicle is at my disposal, I am certainly not unhappy!

However, nothing had prepared me for the regal tour planned for me by the Kadambs. On alighting at the Goa airport, I was taken to their home in Madgaon in their majestic Landcruiser by Bhushan himself. At their home, Bhushan's loving and simple family members, especially his parents who chose to converse in fluent Konkani, made me immediately feel at home. After feasting on a special Konkani breakfast, we set out to tour the Kadamb's properties, with a cavalcade of Landcruisers and Range Rovers (supposedly the best amongst SUVs) trailing behind!

The Kadambs may live simply but the cars in their garage have left me enthralled! The famous Willis Jeep, Mercedes, Hummer and a couple of vintage cars were just some amongst those standing there. Whilst returning, Bhushan himself accompanied me to the airport in a Mercedes CLS.

The original founder of the Kadamb family was Mayur Varmdev, whose throne was originally in Banwasi in Karnataka. The Kadambs ruled over entire Goa and Karnataka.

The head of the Goa branch of the family was Trilochan Kadamb whereas that of the Halshi-Khanpur branch was Gangdev. Banwasi village is located 40 km ahead of Shirsi in Karnataka. There's an idol of Mayur Varmdev to be found here. A throne carved out of a single stone and an exquisite stone temple of Lord Madukeshwar is also found here.

In 1313 A.D, Malik Kafur, the military general of Allauddin Khilji, attacked South India and defeated Ramdevaraya of Devgiri. Later, the Kadambs of Chandrapur – who were then ruling over Goa Pattan i.e. Old Goa – were also attacked by Kafur. The attack led to a few of the Kadambs relocating to Maharashtra and Karnataka.

The ancestor of the Banwasi branch is Shivanand Devraysaheb Kadamb, the father of Bhushan and Atul. Atul has named his son as Jaykeshi, after the first Kadamb king of Goa; whereas the name of Bhushan's son is Veervarmdev, after a Kadamb king of the 10th century. Bhushan's daughter's name is Anishadevi.

The reign of the Kadamb kings was spread over Banwasi, Alshi, Halyal, Bhatkal, Belgaon, Honawar, Ankola, Karwar and Goa. At that time, Honawar was an excellent port from where ivory, spices, sandalwood, peppercorns would be traded to and from Dar-e-salaam, the capital of Tanzania in Africa. The trade in peppercorns especially gained a lot of revenue for the Kadamb kings and their kingdom. One can get a fair idea of their wealth and connections of yore from a glimpse of the invaluable antique ornaments and objects still in possession of the Kadambs. Diamond and emerald necklaces from the Nizams of Hyderabad, priceless carafes from the Ming dynasty a *sher-e-katyar* (gold dagger) and the Kadambs' royal symbol of an eagle created in pure gold are just some of the pieces that I saw. It was the Kadambs' wealth that enabled them to maintain a strong

Sleeping Monk Mountain

naval force of their own. Argaa in Karwar was their main port. It is due to this history that the Indian Karwar naval project has been christened INS Kadamb. Further, the main public vehicular system in Goa is also called Kadamb.

We began visiting their properties in Goa and Karnataka, from Madgaon. Seventy kilometres from Madgaon, is their fort called Sadashivgad. In fact, the village itself is called Sadashivgad. This 'cute-looking' fort is situated on a hillock. Having a strong protective wall and a Mahadarwaza, there's a nice approach road leading towards the fort. It takes 10 minutes to reach the main door from the foothills by car. In the fort, is a resort belonging to the Karnataka Tourism department. There's not much place on the fort but even out of that, 2½ acres is still owned by the Kadambs.

The fort is surrounded by an azure sea with islands dotted by coconut-areca nut trees. One can see a beautiful scenario of a glistening blue sea with a bridge across, from the fort. The famous Devbaug is also seen from the fort.

Statues of horses and horsemen have been intelligently installed outside the fort's protective wall to fool the enemy! There are some small islands around Devbaug. Some of these are privately owned by the Kadambs. One of these islands extends over 7 acres and has a beautiful private beach attached. International celebrities

THE ROYAL KADAMB FAMILY OF MADGAON

like Steven Seagal, Samantha Fox and Richard Gere have visited this island.

I developed special attachment to Sadashivgad because in 1653, Chhatrapati Shivaji Maharaj had toured Belgaon, Karwar and Dharwad and had come to Sadashivgad. He acquired the Shiveshwar fort at Karwar during this tour; where he also paid obeisance to Lord Shivnath. Then, he also acquired the Mirjaan fort which then marked the boundary of Goa. Following that, he conquered the Basavraj fort by sea and went on to Basrur from there. After a series of such glorious accomplishments in the South, he returned to Raigad via the same route.

After visiting Sadashivgad, we travelled 10 km to Karwar for lunch. We feasted on a variety of delicious fish such as Mudadushi (lady fish), Viswan/Surmai (king fish), Tisrya/Shimple (clams), Khekde (crab), Baangde (mackerel), Tarle (sardines) etc at Bharat Vernekar's 'Amruta' restaurant. It was a memorable feast indeed!

From there, we travelled 96 km to the coast to Ankola. It was a fabulous sight to see the hill flanked by the sea-coast, looking like an eagle poised for flight. The sunset looked especially appealing at this place. I was awe-struck to know that this entire property belonged to the Kadambs!

From there, our next stop was the coast of Honawar, located 155 km from Madgaon. An isolated coastal strip stretching 15-16 km long; azure waters, a 51 acre wide island with a fort atop, which can be reached only via boats...such was the beauty of Honawar. Bhushan informed me that this fort was the Basavraj fort that Shivaji Maharaj had visited and consecrated a temple devoted to Goddess Bhawani. The sea-coast here is called as Haldipur beach. The Basavraj sea coast has a nice protective wall and a fresh-water tank.

I asked Bhushan, "If all this is your private property, why don't you develop it to increase tourism potential?"

He answered, "People like you should come forward and do it; we are always there to help."

Amongst their many properties, I liked the mountain shaped like a sleeping man best. It is located 23 km from Karwar and aptly named 'Sleeping Monk'. It is unbelievable how the mountain has been created by nature to resemble an actual man in a sleeping position, pat down to its eyes, ears, folded arms, legs etc. Every year, during Kartik Purnima (full moon day in month of Kartik), there's a fair arranged here. Devotees offer flowers and place lamps near the monk's feet at that time.

The mountain is a natural wonder, reminiscent of the Duke's Nose in Lonavala. One goes into a welcome trance in the company of this mountain, the beautiful river flowing alongside, the coconut and areca nut orchards and the surrounding dense forest.

I had only read or heard about the royal families like Chalukya, Rashatrakut, Shilahar, Kadamb, Satvahan etc; but to associate with an heir (albeit dressed in civil attire) of one of those families was no less than a treat for me!

It remains to be seen when this scenic place on the border of Goa and Maharashtra gets developed as a tourist locale. The Kadambs have already initiated efforts in the direction; I'm sure their efforts will bear sweet fruit!

2. The Bubbly Reservoir of Netravali

While I'm a partial 'Govekar' (belonging to Goa) due to my mother being a Goan native, I was unaware of many unique places in Goa till I shot here for *Bhatkanti*. Earlier, most of my visits to Goa would be spent in visiting relatives with hardly any time left for exploring the place. During the shoot however, I got to see the paintings at Pansaimalsange in the Saange taluka, drawn by the prehistoric man, thousands of years back! I had heard about a pond located in Chandrapur-Gadchiroli area, whose water bubbles vigorously when you clap your hands over it. I came to know of a similar such pond located 52 km away from Madgaon, in front of the Gopinath temple near the Netravali village. During a recent visit to the Akhil Saraswat Samaj conference, the sponsor's son Aditya Angle and his friend enthusiastically agreed to show me that pond.

We reached Netravali from Madgaon in 1-1½ hours. There's also the beautiful Salavli dam further down this road. The vehicle reaches straight up to the temple. Due to the surrounding foliage and lack of residents, the ambience is serene. On the temple itself, is a board proclaiming, "Shri Gopinath Prasanna – Budbud Tale". Obviously my curiosity was piqued.

NETRAVALI'S BUBBLING WATERS

Climbing down a few steps, we reached the pond. Bubbles akin to the one we see in fish-tanks, were arising from various spots in the water. At first glance it seemed that the bubbles were a result of the air present at the bottom of the pond. But there was no sulphuric odour wafting, as it does at Vajreshwari or Sativali. So, this was definitely not a sulphuric gas. We all started clapping loudly near the water's surface.

Netravali Tank

One thing is for sure: while initially after we clapped, there was no change in the speed or quantum of the bubbles rising; yet after a few seconds, the speed and quantum both multiplied vigorously. We experimented by clapping at various spots, only to encounter the same phenomenon at each place. So even if there's any connection of sound-waves with these rising bubbles – one couldn't verify. The temple's priest reaffirmed this possibility, adding that instead of clapping if one loudly chanted 'Om' near the surface, a similar phenomenon would be witnessed.

We tried doing so but couldn't get any results. But it is a good place to view scenic beauty and experience a natural miracle.

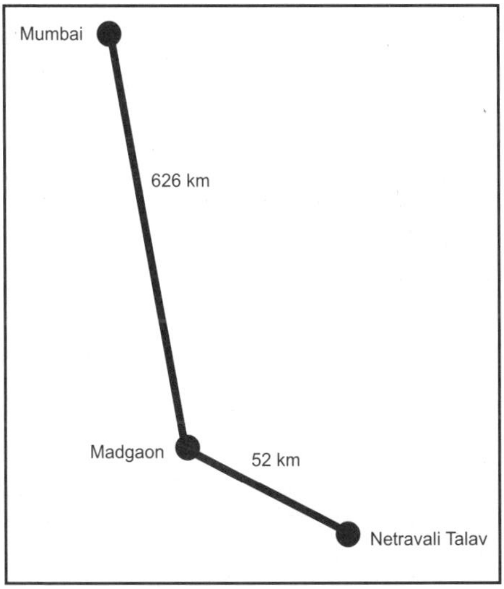

3. Terekhol

Near the border of Maharashtra, just 37 km from Sawantwadi, there's a fort called Terekhol. Terekhol is actually the name of a river which is also the northern border of the state of Goa. The fort is also in Goa state. But the route to go to this fort comes via Sindhudurg district in Maharashtra. The construction of this fort, located among casuarina trees, was done by the Marathas at the beginning of the 18th century. In 1746, the Portuguese captured the fort. In 1794, the Marathas won it back but only for a short while after which the Portuguese snatched it again. It continued to stay with the Portuguese till the time Goa got freedom!

Once the Portuguese felt that a native should be made Governor. Thus the post came to Dr. D'Silva in 1825. But, he began instigating the locals against the Portuguese themselves from this very fort! Obviously the rebellion was crushed and there was tremendous bloodshed in the fort. Dr D'Silva proved the first and last native Governor in Portuguese rule!

Another bloody incident that this fort witnessed was during the Goa Mukti Sangram (Goa Freedom Movement) when some freedom-fighters hoisted the national flag over the fort. At that time, the Portuguese murdered Tulshidas Hirve and Sheshnath Wadekar of Panvel over here.

From the peak of the fort, one can view the exquisite coastal beauty of Goa. The barges and boats with sails that cross over the river to the coast look riveting.

After traversing through an excellent road and crossing a beautiful garden in front of the doorway, we come to the main entrance. It's a formidable door, with pointed iron nails driven into it. The bastions in this fort are very different those found usually in Maharashtra's forts; these have a unique Portuguese architectural style.

Inside, is an ancient church of St Anthony. Be it Portuguese or the British, they both came to India armed with a sword, weighing scales and a Bible! They turned rulers even as they traded here and soon, by brute force, turned religious zealots.

It seems surprising to see a hotel in this fort! In 1976, when Shashikala Kakodkar was the Chief Minister of Goa, this new change was introduced. Now, there's also a resort belonging to Ruben Gama in the fort. But thanks to these developments, the fort is being maintained properly. The fort is located near the Redi village of Sindhudurg. Hence, it is easy for tourists coming to Sindhudurg, to visit this fort. There are buses plying from Sawantwadi and there are good arrangements for lodging and food at the fort.

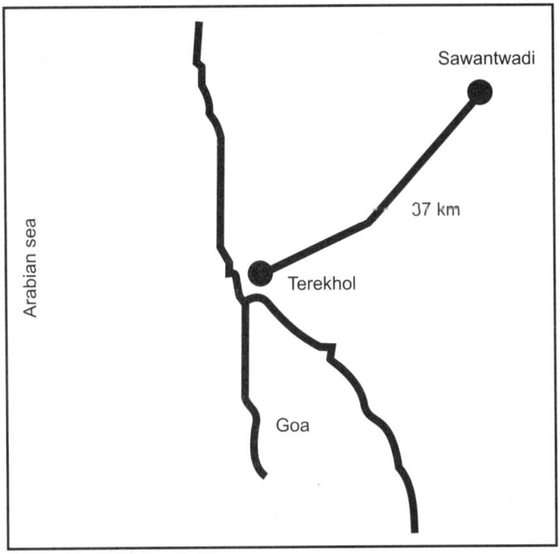

THE STATUE OF JESUS WITH A SIMILAR CLOUD FORMATION

4. Swapnagandha and Wildernest Resort

Two 'dreamers' have joined hands to acquire 450 acres at Goa and have erected a private sanctuary on this land to preserve the flora and fauna. The sanctuary has been aptly named 'Swapnagandha'. Now, they have built the 'Wildernest resort' in Swapnagandha.

This story dates some fifteen years ago! Some 'zapped' nature-lovers were sitting on 'Lasni Temb', a mountain peak at an altitude of 817 m from sea-level. There was just one dream: to preserve the Mhadei sanctuary of Goa, the then-proposed Bhimgad sanctuary of Karnataka and the 450 acre strip of land traversing the middle of jungles then under the jurisdiction of Maharashtra's forest department. In order to preserve the foliage, wilderness and mineral wealth of the area from depletion as also plunder by ruthless contractors, they were dreaming of buying this entire land and converting it into a sanctuary.

Today, after untiring efforts of fifteen years, the dream has finally manifested into reality as Swapnagandha Valley which is located barely 1½ km from Goa. The valley stands miraculously devoid of any urban commotion – soaking in the natural sights, sounds and smells. While unifying itself with the surrounding nature, the valley also allows guests at the Swapnagandha and Wildernest resort, located within the sanctuary, to soak in the experience themselves. Both these resorts are located close to each other. From both resorts, one can get a fabulous view of the valley below. Swapnagandha gives a great view of the reservoir in the valley.

The dream-carvers of this project are Captain. Nitin Dhond and environmentalist Nirmal Kulkarni. Captain Dhond saved penny by penny of his salary to purchase this 450 acre land piece by piece. Whereas Nirmal Kulkarni spent not one, not two but five whole years, traversing the length and breadth of this area, talking to villagers and explaining the importance of environmental preservation. Thus, for five years, while on one hand the land was being acquired bit by bit; on the other hand, the uneducated villagers were being enlightened to stop the perils caused by deforestation and mining. Today, both these efforts have borne fruit. Swapnagandha, the sanctuary has provided much-needed respite for natural resources and the Wildernest Nature resort follows the globally-acclaimed concept of 'eco-tourism'.

Elaborating about the generation of the idea of this resort, Nirmal said, "Swapnagandha is a private sanctuary but funds are very necessary to maintain this place. In the initial days, money was needed

View from Ratnadurg Fort

Chandoli Dam

Birthplace of Shivaji Maharaj, Shivneri

Raigad

to plant trees in deforested areas; to restore the spoilt beauty of the land that had been severely plundered for bauxite, basalt and other minerals; and to especially preserve the rare and exotic medicinal plants, animals, birds and insects in the area. However, if the local *adivasis* (tribals) were not to hunt or mine, how were they to earn their livelihood? It was from this thought that we started the Swapnagandha and Wilderness Nature resort."

The resort became functional three years back. It is now equipped with 18 eco-huts, restaurants, a conservation centre, an *ayurshala* (school for herbal medicine), garden bars called Cloud 9 and Ha, a Cascading Swimming Pool and an Infinity Swimming Pool that seems to touch the horizon. The Log Huts erected here give the guest an experience of staying in a forest; whereas the view of the huge waterfall is stunning to say the least!

When we reach there, a hornbill's pronounced screech signals our arrival! We cannot take our car inside. Escorts dressed as commandoes, take us inside in a military-green jeep. We don't even realise how the pure and unpolluted air fills each cell of our body with a divine kind of freshness. The quietude here is so pronounced that even a rustle of a leaf gets magnified hundred times over. Thus, it is no surprise that we're awoken early in the morning by no alarms but the pitter-patter of dew-drops and chirping of birds! The wind whooshes around languidly – causing the leaves to sway, their rustle inspiring one to set out for a walk in the wilderness!

There are lots of avenues available for a trek/walk here. There are *machans* (observation platforms) erected at many spots in the jungle to enable one to observe the wildlife in seclusion. You can also go for walks through the red-soiled tracks of the Western ghaats, admiring the exquisite flora and fauna. Alternatively, you can go for small treks/hikes or can garner detailed information about the wildlife and foliage here from various experts who are always happy to accompany you.

The resort also invites experts on

various folk-arts to have meaningful interactions with the guests. The resort hosts entertainment programmes wherein one can savour local folk dances etc. The hosts are also equally concerned about preservation and proliferation of such arts and crafts that are on the path to extinction.

The camp fire held at night is a wonderfully joyous experience! The fragrance of fresh local produce being roasted in the fire; folk performances in the backdrop, accompanied by information provided by experts, makes for an interesting confluence of education and entertainment. The food here is very tasty; but you have to forget the taste of Chinese or Continental fare to savour this rustic one to the hilt! Of course, one becomes so unified with nature that such urban tastes are long forgotten! Dig into the sumptuous fare prepared by Ramakant and his assistants and then set out for an exhilarating walk.

On a different note, if, apart from the 'natural intoxication' you want to experience the intoxication that Goa is famed for, visit Cloud 9 – the garden bar! Here, one can taste all kinds of liquors, accompanied by fascinating tales of the jungle, narrated by Bhimnath! If you visit the resort during summer, do not forget to taste the Hurrak – a Goan speciality made from cashews. The wines here are indeed very good. The resort is much patronised by foreign tourists.

All in all, I'm head over heels in love with Swapnagandha sanctuary and Wildernest resort – enriched as they are with over 140 species of birds, innumerable butterflies and animals ranging from a tiny squirrel to tigers!

So, when do you intend to pay a visit?

'Swapnagandha & Wildernest Nature resort'

Address: Swapnagandha, Sankhali, Chorla ghaat, Goa, India.

Email: reservations@wildernest.goa.com

Tel no: 91 9881402665

For reservations: 09341112721, 9341108838

Rates:

Type of Cottage	*Plan*	*How many nights*	*No. of adults*	*Rate*
Forest View	AP	1	2	Rs 3500
Valley View	AP	1	2	Rs 4500
Family Valley View	AP	1	4	Rs 6500

(Rates subject to change)

KONKAN

1. Mochemaad

Place a map of Talkonkan in front of you; close your eyes and let your finger wander over the map and then stop at random. You can be sure that it will be a destination blessed with bountiful natural beauty! Mochemaad is one such tiny village of Talkonkan. Situated very close to Aravalli is Vetoba; this tiny village is an example of an authentic Konkani village.

Mochemaad rests amidst the shade of swaying coconut trees. Houses having red-stone roofs appear to be chatting amidst themselves with their heads bent. No one seems to be in a rush here. Everything is peaceful, slow, serene and calm – the people as also their surroundings. From the backyard, pathways laden with red soil take me towards the sea.

The sea here is a piece of exquisite, untouched beauty with its long, white-sand coast. To use the language of the Sahibs, I'd describe this beach as 'virgin'! During monsoons, I could capture some amazing photos of the coast against a backdrop of grey rain-clouds.

Nestled in the lap of a green hillock, Mochemaad is simply ethereal. The seacoast has trees of kewra (umbrella tree). The bustling waves and untouched coastal strip, made me want to leap for joy like a child!

MOCHEMAAD SEASHORE

One can actually spot starfish here! Biologically belonging to the coelenterata family, this is not really a fish. But yet it is called starfish, due to the way its limbs are created. I caught a starfish in my hand and again let it back on

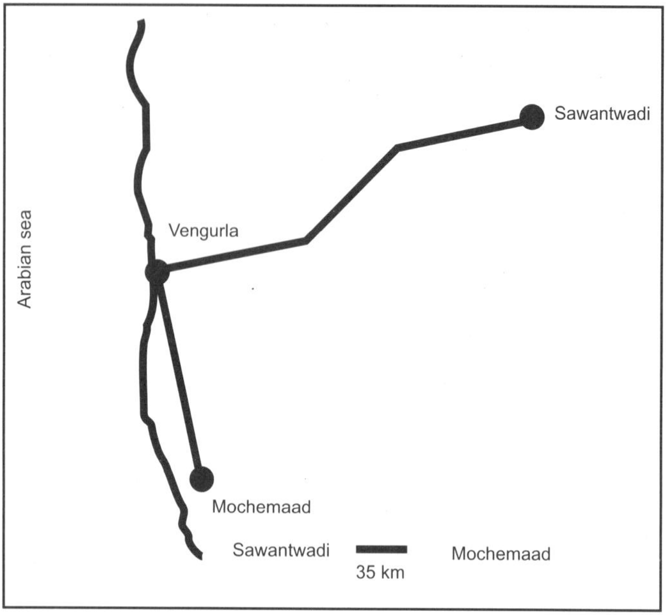
Sawantwadi
Arabian sea
Vengurla
Mochemaad
Sawantwadi
35 km
Mochemaad

Mochemaad

the sand. Surprisingly, it started digging a burrow to hide itself in the sand! In a mere 5-10 seconds it vanished into the sand, leaving a star's imprint behind! There are many such imprints to be found on this coast.

> *Situated very close to Aravalli is Vetoba; this tiny village is an example of an authentic Konkani village.*

Apart from the fisher-folk, Mochemaad is also famous for its 'Dashaavtar artists' (Dashaavtar is a local play based on folk tales and mythology). The talent of Dashaavtari artists from Mochemaad is praised all over Konkan and Goa. To see the exquisite beauty of Mochemaad, one needs to first come to Sawantwadi which is 35 km from here.

Distance: Sawantwadi to Mochemaad – 35 km

ST bus fares for one person:

Mumbai to Mochemaad – Rs 420

Pune to Mochemaad – Rs 360

Nagpur to Mochemaad – Rs 940

Lodging and food: While there's no good arrangement for lodging and food at Mochemaad, which is a small village, nearby Sawantwadi has quite a few good hotels and lodges. These are quite reasonably priced.

It's prudent to stay at Sawantwadi and travel to Mochemaad for sight-seeing.

2. Derwan

About 15-20 years back, the Derwan village in Chiplun taluka was relatively unknown; but today, more and more tourists are including Derwan in their travel-itinerary.

Shri Digambardas Maharaj alias Vitthalrav Ganesh Joshi, (a follower of the Dattatraya sect) initiated the people of Derwan into the joys of spiritualism. He also did a lot of social work with the villagers' assistance. While doing so, he resolved to erect a befitting monument for Chhatrapati Shivaji Maharaj, which resulted in the creation of Shivshrushti. The rationale (or rather the hope) behind Shivshrushti's creation was that it should remind today's self-obsessed Indians of the Chhatrapati's valour and ignite at least a flicker of patriotism in their hearts. Joshi thus wanted to create such magnificent images depicting various scenes from the Chhatrapati's life that the viewer's heart would fill with self-respect and patriotism.

The project slowly materialised. The Shivsamartha Mandir was inaugurated on 5th May, 1981. The work after inauguration was the most tedious one; because the depiction of various scenes and characters from the Chhatrapati's life was still remaining. Slowly, one by one, the requisite characters and scenes came alive. A soldier, a horse-back rider etc got created; after which scenes such as Shivaji's tussle with Shaista Khan; his intelligent tackling of Afzal Khan etc got created. So lively are the creations here that one almost gets transported to that era and feels these things are happening before one's very eyes. The great cultural treasure-trove of Maharashtra – vignettes from the era of Chhatrapati Shivaji – of which all of us should be proud and should preserve carefully to hand over to future generations, is perfectly depicted in the pictorial form at Derwan. The Shivshrushti of Digambardas Maharaj's imagination was realised by the gifted sculptor Dada Patkar and his assistants. Dada Patkar is no longer with us today but the marvellous sculptures that he has created still prove inspiring. The sculptors have poured the elixir of life into the sculptures to depict scenes like the birth of Shivaji Maharaja, the oath-taking ceremony by young Shivaji with his friends at Rohideshwari; the valiant sacrifice given by Bajiprabhu; the grand coronation of Shivaji Maharaja and so on.

Digambardas Maharaj has also erected a monument dedicated to the great saint, creator of Anandvanbhuvan, Shri Ramdas Swami Samarth. This temple contains statues of the Chhatrapati on

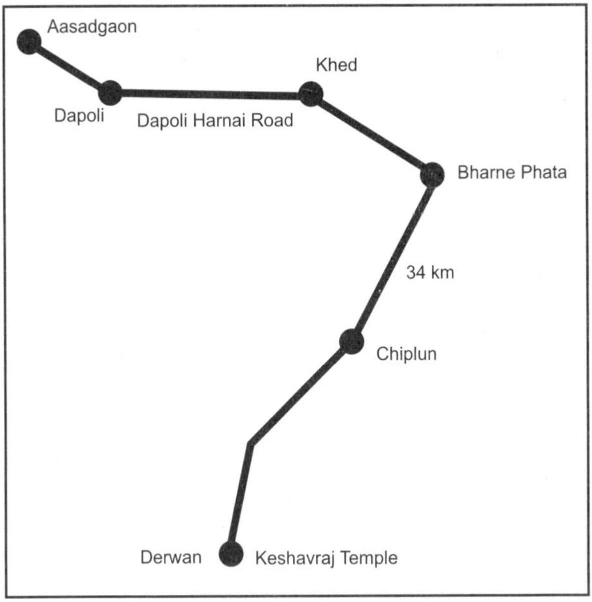

Outside Derwan

horseback, as also of Sant Tukaram, Sant Ramdas and Sant Namdev. Shivsamarth has been constructed akin to a fortress. There are innumerable sculptures of soldiers, men on horseback etc. The pictures and sculptures radiate patriotism – one that we take along with us while leaving.

The great cultural treasure-trove of Maharashtra - vignettes from the era of Chhatrapati Shivaji - of which all of us should be proud and should preserve carefully to hand over to future generations, is perfectly depicted in the pictorial form at Derwan.

Derwan lies on the route going from Chiplun to Ratnagiri, about 9 km from Chiplun. There's a bus available from Chiplun to Ratnagiri. If you take a bus from Ratnagiri, get down at Sawarde. Shivshrushti is 10 minutes by walk from there. One can either come back to Chiplun from Shivshrushti or can proceed to sight-seeing at Ratnagiri.

3. Ratnadurg Fort

Ratnagiri is often fêted as 'Konkan's Treasure-trove' and for reasons more than one. While Ratnagiri is instantly associated with Alphonso mangoes, apart from them too Ratnagiri has a distinctive identity

This famous town has hosted Swatantryavir Sawarkar; has seen Lokmanya Tilak's childhood and has seen the career of Vishnushastri Chiplunkar (known as the Shivaji of Marathi language) flourish.

There are quite a few places in this town to see and savour. We're going to see the jewel in its crown – the Ratnadurg fort. Ratnadurg fort is a water-fort. There's a concretised road up to the fort; so one can take vehicles right upto the entrance. Its circumference is quite huge but apart from the Bhagwati Devi temple, Deepgruh (lighthouse) and a few houses, no ancient construction remains here today.

One can have a panoramic view of the Ratnagiri town from the seven bastions and numerous balconies constructed in the fort's wall. Today, there's water on all three sides of the fort. It is said, that earlier, the fort was surrounded by water on all four sides. But the British filled up the side connecting to the village for easy access and thus water remained on only three sides. Ratnadurg fort has twenty-seven bastions in all. Researchers say that the fort was constructed in the Bahamani era. It later went into the hands of Adil Shah of Bijapur. Chhatrapati Shivaji took over the fort in 1670 and repaired it extensively. Thus, even today the fort's walls are standing as formidable as ever. After Chhatrapati's demise, the fort went into the hands of Siddis, but Kanhoji Angre fought valiantly and won it back.

Ratnadurg Fort

From the many bastions of this huge fort, one can see lots

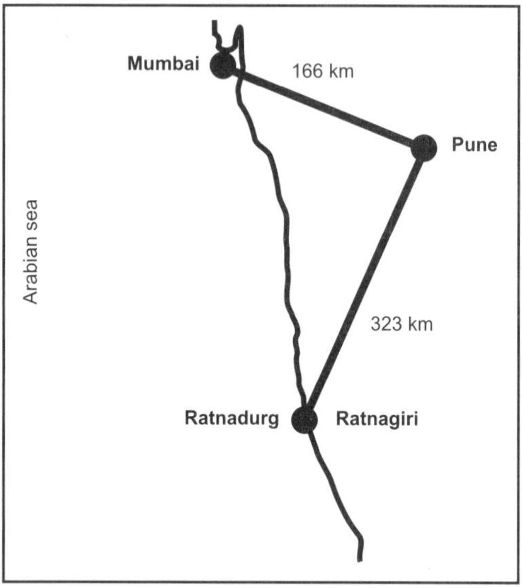

Ratnadurg Fort

of scenic beauty. Today, the fort has become a tourist attraction due to the Bhagwati Devi temple.

While Ratnagiri is instantly associated with Alphonso mangoes, apart from them too Ratnagiri has a distinctive identity.

This Devi is considered the sister of Mahalakshmi Devi. On Mahalakshmi Devi's instructions, Bhagwati Devi slayed the demon Ratnasur who was residing here – or so goes the legend. Though the fort was restored during the Chhatrapati's reign, it was re-consecrated three times. The self-emerged temple of the Devi is 2½ ft tall. The Devi holds a conch, a disc, a sword and a shield – holding which she is sitting atop Mahishasur.

Navratra and Shimga are two main festivals celebrated at this temple. Due to the temple and a trip around the old fort, there are always loads of tourists here. The fort is 15 minutes away from the town and one can reach there by bus or rickshaw.

4. Vijaydurg

Of all the sea-forts of Southern Konkan, my favourite remains the Vijaydurg. The formidable stone walls of the fort, which are still as strong as ever; the fort's strategic location, the view of the red-soil laden pathways, quaint houses and tiny boats bobbing afar in the azure sea, that one can see from the windows in the stone walls, is a photographer's delight. Ninad Bedekar has penned a very informative book on Vijaydurg and was kind enough to give me some very important information about the walls that extend deep into the sea.

One can reach Vijaydurg from Jaitpur by boat – crossing the Baghotan khaadi (creek); or can reach by bus, coming from the Mumbai-Goa expressway, turning towards the right at Talere after Kharepatan. You can also come here by car.

Sealed from three sides by sea-water and containing 27 bastions, Vijaydurg was earlier known as Gheriya. Originally a fort belonging to the Shilaharas, it was later conquered by the Bahamanis and then Adilshah of Bijapur. In 1664, Chhatrapati Shivaji won the fort from Adilshah. During Peshwai (reign of the Peshwas), this fort was an important centre for Kanhoji Angre's naval rule. Later, the fort kept changing hands between the Peshwas and British.

VIJAYDURG FORT

Sindhudurg

Pandavleni, Nashik

Semadoh Sanctuary, Melghat

The wonderous potholes at Nighoj

Seashore at Kunkeshwar

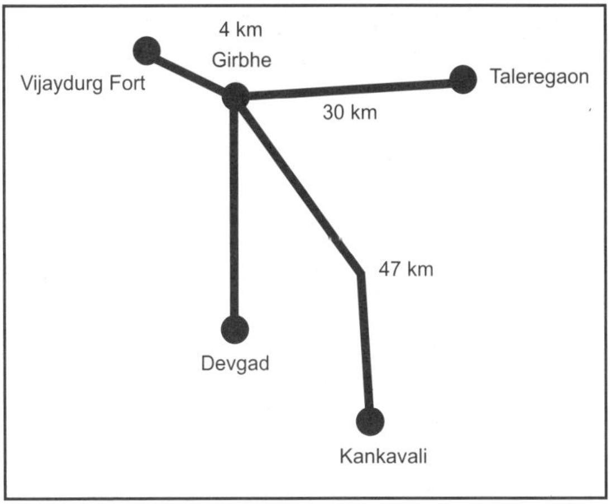

On entering the fort, one first comes across a temple of Shri Hanuman. Crossing three doors, one reaches the main door aka Mahadwar, beyond which is a police station. Over here, one can see cannonballs neatly arranged along the roadside. Nearby, is a two-storeyed building with a basement, the government rest-house. There are concretised ledges opposite this rest-house. In 1897, an astronomer-cum-scientist named Joseph Lockyer had come specially to see the total solar eclipse. The ledges were built to support his special binoculars. It was during his research that helium was discovered.

Close to the ledges, one can see a circular device which was used to crush limestone. Apart from that, one can also see remains of the mint and the ammunition room.

A surprising revelation was recently made about the walls of Vijaydurg. When in the past, British naval ships had come to attack Vijaydurg, they had collided with something and been wrecked. But it was never clear as to what exactly they had collided with. Recently, naval officer Commander Gupchup dived deep into the water with his assistants and found a strong wall erected deep under the sea, dating almost 300 years back i.e. during the reign of Chhatrapati Shivaji! The wall is so deep down that it is not visible even during low tide! Well-known for making his enemies quake in their boots due to his amazing guerrilla warfare on land, this idea of Shivaji Maharaja's to protect the sea-fort is unmatched in its ingenuity!

Apart from this, one can also see a huge naval dock built during Kanhoji Angre's reign, close by in the Girye village and a temple of Shri Rameshwar, located just 3 km before reaching Vijaydurg.

5. Keshavraj Temple

The monsoon clouds have just descended on the Arabian Sea. The rains are pouring down over Konkan. It was on one such rainy day, on a rainy way, that we set out for yet another beautiful destination in Konkan.

The rain took a small hiatus and I ventured out to climb down a few stone steps to enter a small settlement - with huts made of thatch roofs – called Dabkewadi. Two women were busy sorting grain in the courtyard of one such house. The grains dancing in their grain-sieve were creating a joyous rhythm. I asked them if I was on the right road. Without lifting their heads, they nodded a yes and off I marched ahead, with the grain still dancing rhythmically.

Till then, I had seen much of what Konkan has to offer but the untouched, ethereal Konkan that I had read about in the books of GoNiDa (G.N. Dandekar) and Pendse (S.N. Pendse) was being witnessed by me for this first time in this area. The pebbled pathway was flanked by areca trees. Competing with each other to touch the sky, the trees were drenched with rain-water. Droplets of water, slipping off their shiny leaves, were disappearing into the red earth. Somewhere in between, jackfruit trees, heavily laden with fruit, were also making their presence felt. Those trees were looking like a fond father standing with kids nestled lovingly in his arms.

This area is the area of Aasud, mentioned in S.N. Pendse's novel "Gaarambicha Bapu". The novel depicts Konkan as it was 50-60 years back. Surprisingly, the description fits the places one sees on the way to Keshavraj, even today – so untouched and unchanged is the beauty of this part of Konkan. Even though Keshavraj is a bit off the main road, tourists make it a point to come here. Walking a bit ahead on the pebbled walkway, one comes across a small, bubbly rivulet. Earlier, there was a bridge to cross this rivulet but now it is broken. We were told that plans are afoot to soon build a concrete bridge over here. Since there was little water in the river, I could easily go across on foot. It was mesmerising to see the water jauntily travelling with me over the pebbles. I sat down on a rock, for a brief rest. The serene orchards of coconut and areca-nuts; the lush green hillock of Keshavraj standing nearby; the human settlements far away and water teasing my feet as it runs ahead over the pebbles. At such times, one tends to forget one's own self! Our existence becomes but a small droplet on nature's canvas. The delicate waves on the clear water were creating deep impressions on my heart

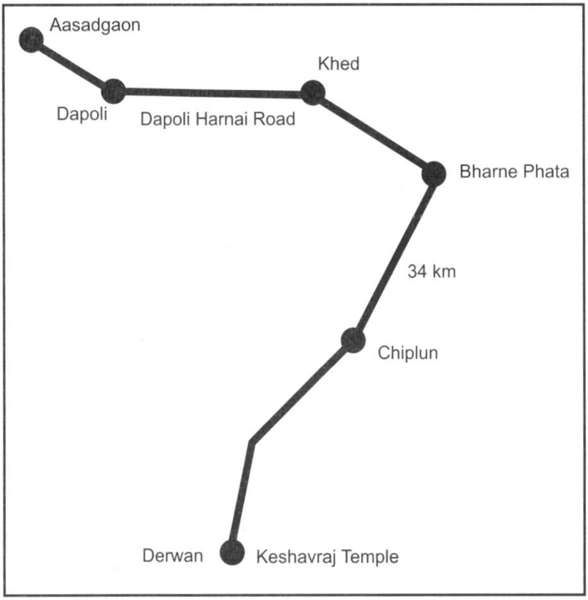

KESHAVRAJ TEMPLE

and mind. Finally, I came out of my reverie, only to realise that there was a lot more to conquer on the way.

The steep slopes slowly gave way to small steps. On running up the steps I saw ripe berries decorating their shrubs. Was it possible that I could go ahead without feasting on this bounty of nature? Rather than buying it in the market, the joy of plucking and feasting on these berries in the wild, is an incomparable joy! A sappy fluid flows out of the berries and leaves a tingling, satisfying sensation on the tongue. After tasting the berries, I climbed a bit ahead and reached the temple. The temple has a small entrance. Inside, a constant stream of water falls into the stone-vessel from a *gomukh* (cow-mouth). This water has been brought down from a stony ravine. Hats off to the genius who thought of this idea! After washing my feet in this cold water, I went in to pay obeisance to Lord Keshavraj. The temple is quite simple. But the cleanliness in the surroundings enhances the simple beauty of the place. The frontal hall has a tin-roof. The sanctum sanctorum is quite dark but the idol is visible in the mild light spread by the laamandiva (brass lamp on a chain). The idol is a carved out from black stone and holds a conch, lotus, disc and mace – from which one presumes that it is an idol of Lord Vishnu's Keshav figure.

A visit to Shri Keshavraj in the serene, beautiful natural surroundings proves unforgettable. Aasud is located 7 km on the Dapoli-Harnai route. Get down near the Aasud garden just before Vyaghreshwari. If you cross the river near Dabkewadi and climb up the steps going through the dense forest, Keshavraj is located a mere ½ an hour away.

SANGLI AND KOLHAPUR DISTRICT

1. Koynanagar

Amongst the few upcoming scenic locales in India, one can particularly look forward to Koynanagar. The reason for using the term 'upcoming' for Koynanagar is that although the Koyna dam and the huge backwaters behind this dam on the Koyna river are well-known, earlier there were not many conveniences available to enable tourists to spend a couple of days in this naturally-gifted locale. Of course, the MTDC resort was always there. But lately, the Minister of Environment, a descendant of the Patan family, Vikramsinghji Patankar, took a lead in starting many beneficial projects here. These initiatives have resulted in Koynanagar turning into a mini-Mahabaleshwar of sorts!

Apart from Koynanagar's holiday resort, Vikramsinghji also has his own Wind Chalet resort here. The waters of Koyna run as high as 2000 ft. The Wind Chalet resort is located 800 ft high on the mountain behind the dam. The MTDC resort is also situated close by. An observation point has been created. A fountain has been erected close-by. I got an opportunity to see the surroundings of the -resort with Vikramsinghji himself. I reached Satara after a 260 km-long trip from Mumbai. There are two ways to go to Koynanagar from Satara. One way goes from Satara via Karad and Patan to Koynanagar. The other goes from the mountain which hosts the Sajjangad fort; crossing over the waterfall of Thoseghar or Chalkewadi and reaches Koynanagar via Patan. Patankar deliberately took me via the second route to see the 950-odd windmills located on a 3500 ft high plateau behind Chalkewadi. The rotating blades of these windmills look fascinating! Winds rush around at tremendous speed over the plateaus, in all seasons; which is what inspired Vikramsinghji to capitalise on the same to produce electricity by erecting windmills. Initially, technicians were invited from abroad to erect the windmills. Vikramsinghji takes obvious pride and affection in this electricity-manufacturing project which employs no other resources except natural wind! Descending a bit from this windmill project, one comes to a plantation called 'Kaathicha Tek'. Further below is a village called 'Avsari'. Patankar showed me first the beautiful scene of the Koynanagar dam and the swell of the waters of Shivsagar from this point. A 17-18 km patch of road here is quite rocky

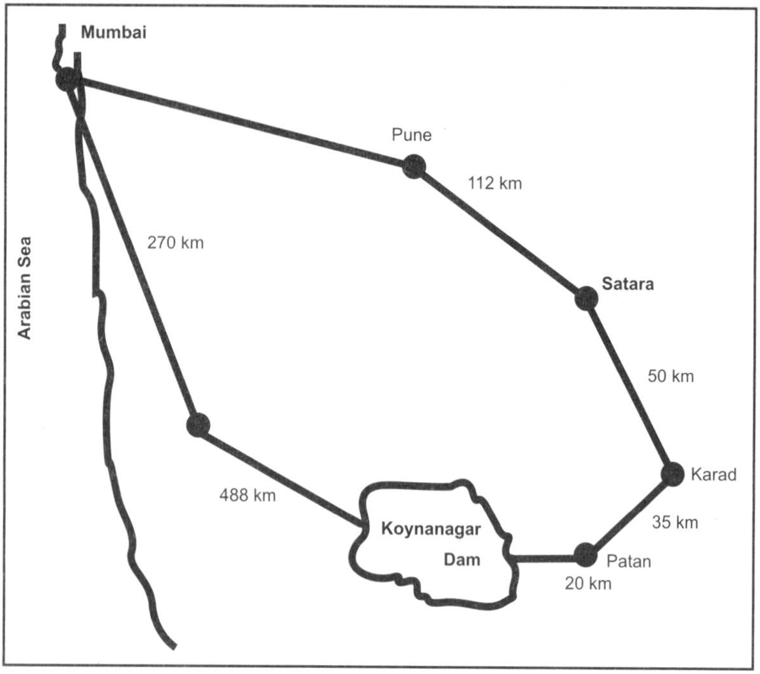

KOYNANAGAR RESERVOIR

but the beginning and the end of the road has been concretised; with plans afoot for the concretisation of the rest of it soon.

After seeing the windmills, we came back to the mansion-like home of the Patankars in Patan. I was overjoyed to see the antique and historically-significant articles in the house. Ancient historical notes, pictures of regally-draped ancestors standing tall with swords or guns in hand, heirloom furniture, weapons, utensils etc seen in the house, sent a unique excitement coursing through me. Particularly mentionable is the Ram mandir (temple of Lord Rama) situated in the house. The temple is preserved and immensely cared for. The silver idol of Lord Rama in this temple has been given by none other than Samarth Ramdas Swami himself! I was also fortunate to see letters written by Chhatrapati Shivaji Maharaj to the ancestors of Vikramsinghji!

After a wonderful tea-session, we travelled 20 km to reach Koynanagar. Night is not the best time to roam around Koynanagar, whose fragmented and uneven geographical terrain makes it difficult to chart a journey therein.

For dinner, we enjoyed the local speciality of tambda rassa (red mutton gravy) and fresh pomfret that came straight from Chiplun in Konkan, located just 48 km away from Koynanagar.

I woke up early in the morning at 6 am and was dazzled by the sight in front of my European cottage! The Shivsagar reservoir was gleaming red and gold with the sun-rays bouncing off its shimmery surface. The waters thus 'aflame' made a striking contrast with the dark mountain ranges and the red and gold sky above – an artist's delight! Whilst admiring this sight, I saw two air-jets zoom across the sky, seemingly towards the sun, from amidst the dark clouds, leaving a snowy trail behind. I couldn't resist capturing the sight on camera! Gradually, the sun began rising to reveal the surroundings, including the European-styled Wind Chalet, in all its splendour. This chalet has been built using earthquake-resistant techniques and plans are afoot to build 4-5 similar such chalets.

The temperature was around 15-16 degree Celsius and thus, very pleasant and cool. Vikramsinghji, his son Satyajit, a colleague Rajabhau Kale and I, all descended the small ghaat to sit in the 'Nisargakanya' launch, standing at one side of the dam. Generally, one has to scream to make oneself heard whilst chatting in a launch. In fact, I sometimes wonder, why do people even attempt to talk whilst in a launch or in a discotheque! But the engine of this launch was so gentle that we had a hearty chat all the way! The circumference of the Shivsagar reservoir is quite large. The distance, if measured from the wall of the Koynanagar dam to Tapola (on a bypass of Mahabaleshwar) is approximately 65 km It takes around 3¼ hours to traverse the distance by a launch.

Numerous branches of the Sahyadri range have entered the basin of Shivasagar. These include hidden forts like Wasota. One can see dense forestation beginning from the foothills of every mountain that begins from the basin of Shivsagar, right up to its peak. Such thick forests are rarely seen elsewhere in Maharashtra. Leopards, tigers, wild boars, antelopes, deer and such other wild animals inhabit these jungles and if you're lucky, you may spot one of these drinking water at the reservoir early in the morning. Animals such as the Indian Giant Squirrel and porcupine, and colourful birds like the Hornbill, Parakeets, Paradise Fly-catcher, Hoopoe etc are also spotted here. The waters of Shivsagar host ample freshwater fish such as Catla, Maral and Rohu.

It was a thrilling experience to listen to the tales of shikaars (hunts) done here by the ancestors of Patankar – more so because we had tethered the launch nearby and were sitting in the dense forest wherein these shikaars had taken place!

One can see tents erected at some spots near the water. We did not go all the way to Tapola but instead, after a 2-2½ hour excursion, came back to Patan. One can see photographs and films providing valuable information about the dam-project in a hall at the beautifully-constructed Nehru Garden, near the dam. There are amazing clusters of roses and other flowers in this garden. It also has playthings and games for children. Valuable thoughts and sayings by Pt. Nehru have been carved on stones here.12 km from the dam; we can see a waterfall called Ozarde. Cascading from a height of 800 ft, it is amongst the biggest waterfalls in Maharashtra – or, so can be safely surmised. This waterfall overflows beautifully during and after the monsoons. Also 10 minutes from the resort is the Model Room. Here, one can get detailed information about the Koyna hydro-electric project. Further, it is worth seeing the production of rattan chairs (a material made from a species of palm akin to bamboo) and herbal medicines made by a voluntary organisation located in the dam's surroundings. Patankar himself is also quite well-versed in the qualities of various medicinal plants. A women's voluntary organisation located nearby makes delicious pickles, papads and crunchies to take home as mementoes.

Some more scenic sports near Koynanagar - Morgiri, Gheradategad (fort), Dhareshwar deul (temple) are good places for trekkers. One can reach Koynanagar in an hour's time from Konkan via Mumbai-Goa expressway or by the Konkan Express train from Chiplun. The distance between Chiplun and Koynanagar is barely 48 km. One can also check out the Shivshrushti at Derwan near Chiplun, if so inclined. Also, the bird sanctuary created by Vikramsingh's uncle, 3 km from Patan, is also worth visiting.

All in all, on visiting Koynanagar, I strongly felt that it will not take time before the place gets converted to resemble Mahabaleshwar, which lays barely 4½ hours away via boat through the Shivsagar dam. By road, the journey takes around 5½ hours via the Satara-Karad route. It is a great place for tourists to visit for 3-4 days. The best time to come is during monsoons and the 3-4 months after monsoons.

The letter written by Chhatrapati Shivaji Maharaj to an ancestor of Vikramsinghji Patankar:

श्री

स्वस्ति श्री राज्याभिषेक शके ४ पिंगळ नाम संवस्सरे माघ शुद्ध द्वादशी गुरुवार क्षत्रिय कुलावतंस श्री राजा शिवछत्रपती यांनी बाळाजीराव धादाजीराव परगणे पाटण यांना पुढील प्रमाणे आज्ञा केली असे तुम्ही पाठविलेले पत्र मिळाले व आपले तपशिलास (सविस्तर) वर्तमान समजले तेव्हा तुम्ही मानाचे धनी (मान मिळविण्यात योग्य) आणि वतनी (ज्यांना वतन किंवा वृत्ती दिली आहे असा) आज्ञात तुमच्यावर स्वामी (श्री शिवाजी महाराज) यांची कृपा आहे लढाईत यशवंत रावाना वीर मरण आले तरी त्यांची आयुष्य मर्यादा तितकीच होती. त्यास काय उपाय? तुम्ही त्यांच्या मुलांची विचारपूस करीत जावी त्यांचे (यशवंतरावाचे) पांडे वगैरे त्याचे मुलाचे नावे करून पूर्वीच पत्राद्वारे पाठविले आहे व राजमान्य आनावी दत्तो यांना त्यांची विचारपूस होऊन त्याप्रमाणे तह हयात त्यांची वृत्ती (सरंजाम) चालू ठेवावा आपले समाधान होईल (आपला कारभार आमप्रकारे चालेल) असे करण्याबाबत ---- अनाजी पंतास पत्र लिहून कळविले आहे लेखनालंकार

भवदीय विराजते

MORGIRI FORT

2. Amboli

A few years back I decided to explore the Sindhudurg district. From Kolhapur I went to Gadhinglaj and from there I started off via Amboli Ghaat to tour the district. Sindhudurg is the first district in Maharashtra to be recognised as a tourism district. Every village in this district is a tourist spot in itself. A beauteous and long coastal strip, dotted with sea forts, islands, imposing mountains decorated with trees of various kinds and the serene, lovely temples in almost all the villages, ensure a throng of tourists to Sindhudurg. The warm welcome in Malwani (Sindhudurg's native dialect) makes you feel instantly at home. The tasty seafood obtained from the foaming sea, leaves an unforgettable taste on one's tongue! So come along; the land keeps calling, saying, *"Yeva, Konkan aaplach asa!* (Welcome, Konkan is all yours!)"

Situated at an approximate altitude of 2000 ft. and blessed with the scenic beauty of Konkan and the cool breeze of the ghaats, Amboli is a cool place in the Sindhudurg district. The Amboli ghaat is on of the ancient routes used to descend into Konkan.

The Hiranyakeshi River has its origin on a hillock that one encounters whilst coming to Amboli via the Gadhinglaj route from Kolhapur. That is where the river originates from beneath a rock.

Near the origin of Hiranyakeshi river is a cave. One can go deep into the cave but it is immensely dark inside. Some people from Kolhapur tried to unravel more about this cave in the past and found that there are seven hot-water springs in this cave. But due to the lack of oxygen, a very narrow pathway and the overpowering stench, they had to turn back before they could find anything more.

Ragheshwar Math: About 2 km down the river's coast is situated the Ragheshwar Math. It gets its name from Ragheshwar of Kolhapur, the founder of this Math. Its peace and quietude has mesmerised even the biggest of saints and pious men. Ragheshwar Math is located 5 km from Amboli, which itself is situated 84 km from Kolhapur. This riverside Math saw the installation of a beautiful idol of Shri Rama in 1997. The idol of the 'kodandadhari' (bow-carrying Shri Rama) is very serene and captivating.

Naagachya Murti: One can see the rarely found naag-murtis (snake idols) at this place. Naagdevta (the Snake-God) is fabled to reside in the nether-lands. The hood of the Snake-God is said to carry the world and thus, the Snake-God has for long been worshipped in India.

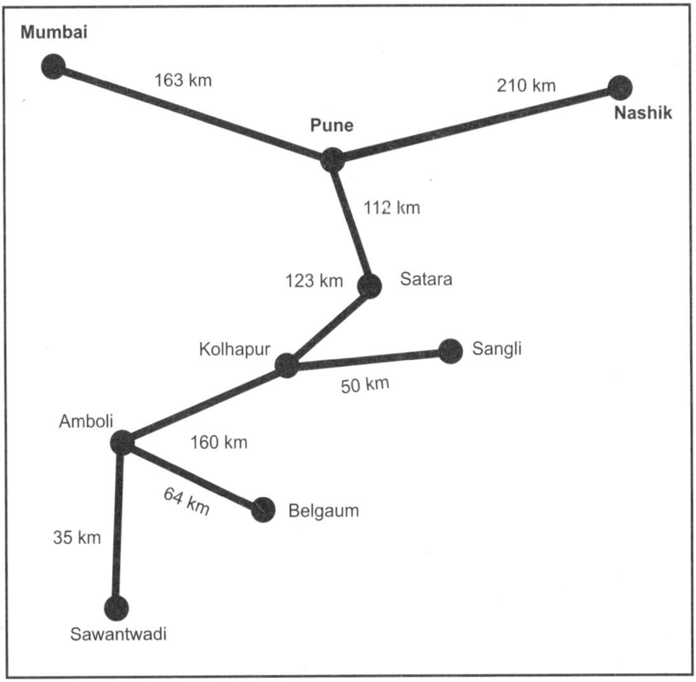
Mumbai
163 km
210 km
Nashik
Pune
112 km
123 km
Satara
Kolhapur
Sangli
50 km
Amboli
160 km
64 km
Belgaum
35 km
Sawantwadi

AMBOLI

Swayambhu Ganpati: A boulder located near the riverbed, is a self-created Ganesha idol. If you observe it closely Ganesha's trunk is clearly visible on the boulder. Devotees throng to seek the blessings of this Ganesha.

Shivling: Devotees have installed a Shivling (an oblong stone sculpture representing Lord Shiva) in a small marble temple near the origin of Hiranyakeshi. This Shivling is also said to be self-created.

Mahadevgad: This is considered to be the most beautiful spot in Amboli. One can see lush greenery all around from the mountain peak. A part of the mountain range has got separated from Mahadevgad and looks like it is rushing to dissolve into the horizon! The natural folds on the mountains give them a unique texture. The greenery looks exquisitely varied due to the same reason. We are well-acquainted with renowned hill-stations like Matheran and Mahabaleshwar but Amboli is equally beautiful. The long and sturdy railing, built here for tourists' safety, can be called a speciality of this point.

Shirgaonkar Point: About 3 km after turning left from the highway, is the Shirgaonkar Point. One can experience the rare sight of lush greenery upto wherever one's vision reaches, at this point. Looking below from this point, one can see the captivating sight of the reddish snaking road, making a sharp contrast with the greenery around.

Ghaatatla mandir (temple in the ravines): This small temple has been created by erecting a small shed on the ghaat-road. A God by the interesting name of 'Shri Dev Purvicha Vas ki Purvas' resides in this temple. Every ghaat has a temple where the ghaat begins. Drivers halt for a small break near these temples to pray for a safe journey and to check the brakes etc.

Sunset point: Nestled amidst the mountain ranges of Amboli, is the Sunset Point. It's an exhilarating experience to see the sun set beyond the lush greenery and mountains. From the Sunset point, it appears as if the western horizon is alit with the 'Flame of the Forest' flowers! The entire horizon looks ruby-red in colour and the heart hums these poetic verses in Marathi, which perfectly recreate the ambience:

"Meghanchya astaavar palsaancha jaal;
Astaachya kanthat maankanchi maal"

Sunset is the best time to view this beauty to the optimum.

3. Kaaplingeshwar

Recently, I got an opportunity to shoot for a regional Marathi movie called 'Paisa Kari Salaam' at a picturesque village called Paatpanhala, situated on the road going towards Anuskura ghaat on the Kolhapur-Gaganbawda road. I've played a body-builder/wrestler in this movie based on Mr Dalvi's award-winning book, *Jigar*.

During shooting, the arrangements for our residence were made at the palatial bungalow of Rajabhau Khanvilkar (brother of Digvijay Khanvilkar). At night, Rajabhau and his friends Akolkar, Nanivadekar and I would spend the time chatting.

Beyond this village surrounded by mountains lies a dense forest. The Konkani* beauty of red soil and lush green mountains combines with the cool breeze blowing in this region located between the two ghaats, Anuskura and Gaganbavda, to lend a unique beauty to this place. The Mhasai plateau, which forms an important juncture of the Panhalgad-Vishalgad trek, is also seen from here. Initially I thought that this place is called Paatpanhala because it is located behind Panhala; but no reference was found to validate this thought of mine.

The surrounding forts, the dense forests and shikaars (stories of hunting expeditions) used to be the main topics of discussion with Rajabhau and his friends. During one such discussion I found that Kaamlinga, located on a neighbouring mountain is being developed as a tourist spot by the Maharashtra Government. Nearby, is a cascading waterfall called Barki. Hence, I sought out information about these two places from Ravsaheb Patil, a gentleman from Paatpanhala.

Paatpanhala the village is located 34 km to the west of Kolhapur on the Kale-Bhogav route. The Kasari River flows perennially from the north of the village, meandering over the village periphery. From the south of the village flows the Jambhli River, which meets the Kasari River in the north-east. Thus, the village is surrounded by water on three sides and has the formidable Shri Kaaplinga Mountain on the west. Shri Kaaplinga is a sacred place where boons are said to be granted and falls in the Kolhapur district.

Shri Kaaplinga is located at an altitude of 2500 ft. above sea-level. There are two routes to go to Kaaplinga from Paatpanhala village. Both are narrow pathways. One route is the Ambeshet- Payardand-

---

(Konkan is a portion of land at sea level between Sahyadri/Western ghaats. The strip is approximately 40-60 kms wide and extends from Mumbai to Goa. The people and the dialect of the region both are referred to as Konkani).*

Tali route from the south of the village and is 3.5 km long. It doesn't contain any very steep climbs. The other route originates from the west of the village and is called Vetalmaal-Ghatshilicha Tek Takyacha Pani. This route is estimated to be around 2-2.5 km long.

A kilometre-long walk from Vetalmal takes us to the Ghatshila peak. There is sparse forestation on this route. After the 1-2 furlong straight path on the peak, begins the Forest Department's border and thereafter the first point itself, which is a steep slope, tires you out. From here begins a dense forest. There are many berry thickets on this route. Jambhul, Hingal, Ain, Kinjal, Amba, Nana, Hirda, Behda, Aawla, Shisham, Shivan, Payri and other trees are found here. After this point one gets to see the pond. This pond is perennially irrigated due to the springs located in it.

One can spot animals like rabbits and antelopes on this waterfront. Grey jungle fowl are found aplenty here; as are wild boars, porcupines, peafowl, pangolins etc.

Beyond the waterfront, the entire route goes through dense forest. The climb is not very steep on this route. Midway, one enters a sparse forest and then after some time, the Kaaplinga peak (the highest point in this jungle) becomes visible. This entire hillock is covered by dense forest. Via this route, it takes around 1-1 ¼ hour to reach the Kaaplinga temple.

The temple is east-facing and small. The sanctum sanctorum is around 6 by 6 feet wide. The walls of the temple are stone set in limestone and are around 2 feet broad. The main hall rests on wooden pillars and recently, brick and mortar work has been added on the fringes. The tin roof was renewed recently in 2005, on the eve of Mahashivaratri.

There's a small courtyard in front of the temple beyond which one notices dense foliage. There's a tableland to the west. On the left is a sliver of mountain taller than Barki, while the south-east contains a plateau. Of the east-north-east side are Gad-Pavangad and Jotiba. Towards the south-west is the captivating water body of Pombre Paatbandhara. Far away to the east, one can see the valley of Kasari.

People from areas around Paatpanhala flock to it during Mahashivaratri. The nights are enlivened with bhajan-keertan and the programmes ends with the distribution of mahaprasad the next day. Again, during the month of Shravan, people take puranpolis (a sweet delicacy) to Kaaplinga and break their fast there.

On the day of Ashvin Suddha Panchmi, the palanquin of Paatpanhala's village deity Shri Chaturbhuja Devi arrives at Kaaplinga and returns to the village after 12 noon.

The palanquin is given a royal welcome by the villagers, who clean their courtyards, draw rangolis and host the palanquin with reverence and love.

Even local schools of Panhala-Shahuwadi districts organise excursions to this area. This scenic place is being fast developed by the government's tourism department as a tourist destination.

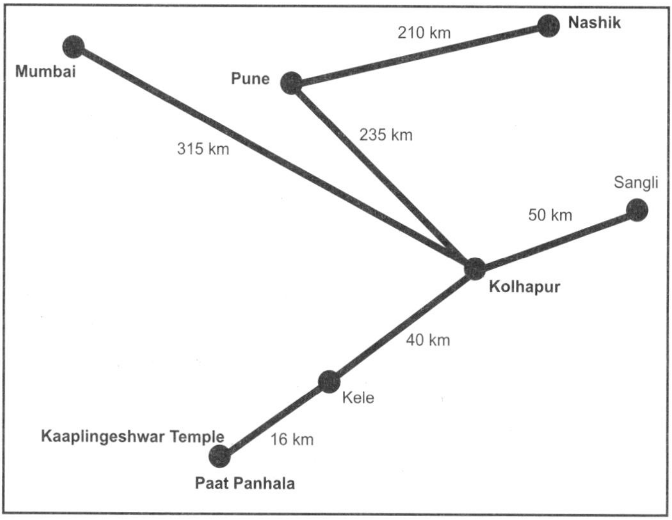

KAAPLINGESHWAR FOREST

4. Barki Waterfalls

Barki village is situated on the Bajar Bhogav-Anuskura route, approximately 18 km from Bhogav and 11 km from Anuskura. From Paatpanhala, this distance becomes 16 km. Blessed with scenic beauty and surrounded by hills and valleys, this is the only village from the Kolhapur district to have been in the Gramdaan movement. There is no gram panchayat here; only a Sarvodaya mandal. This village is situated 3 km from the Kasari river and contains little irrigated agriculture.

Towards the south of the village, is an imposing mountain range on which is located a wide plateau, around 1 km wide and 5-5½ km long. The plateau is surrounded by sharp climbs and below it is a thick forest. In the Shahuwadi-Panhalgad forest range, one can see the rare black bears. Apart from the usual animals, one can also find tigers, deer and boars here.

The Barki plateau is located at an altitude of approximately 3200 ft above sea-level. Towards the west of this plateau, is the scenic Anuskura ghaat. During monsoons, water flows fast from this plateau onto the mountains and then comes out in the direction of Barki as 6-8 waterfalls. Most of these waterfalls are seen from afar only. But the highest waterfall, called Tapera, cascading from a height of 200 ft, is not at all visible until you reach the mouth of the valley. This waterfall is also quite renowned. After being 'discovered' by journalists 4-5 years back, tourists prefer travelling 48 km from Kolhapur to Tapera, instead of going 90 km to Amboli. During monsoons, 1000-1500 tourists flock here every weekend. Barki is situated around 16 km from Paatpanhala and Tapera is 1 km away from Barki. Anuskura ghaat is 11 km from Barki. Pavankhind is located 36 ms from Paatpanhala on the Yelvan-Jugaai route; whereas Pavankhind is 13 km away from Malkapur. Barki is 38 km from Malkapur.

In this area, food is best available at Bajarbhogav-Kale-Malkapur whereas lodging can be found only at Amba in the Kolhapur-Malkapur area.

The Vashi bus is available from Kolhapur's Rankalves bus stand to go to Paatpanhala at 8.30 am, 1.30 pm and 6.00 pm. The whole road is tarred. Kumbhavde, Burambal buses go ahead from the Paatpanhala paati and Barki paati. In recent times, the Rajapur-Kolhapur bus has begun a service on this route via Pachal, Anuskura and Bhogav.

The water-bodies present in this area and their approximate sizes are as follows:

1) The Bajiprabhu pond located at their foot of Vishalgad on the Kasari River is 3.5 TMC. The dam department has a rest house here.

2) The Kumbhavde pond is located on Gaavdi river and is 1 TMC.
3) Gaavdi pond is also located on Gaavdi River and further meets the Kasari River.
4) Padsali and Pombre ponds are located on Jambhli River which is a subsidiary of the Kasari River.

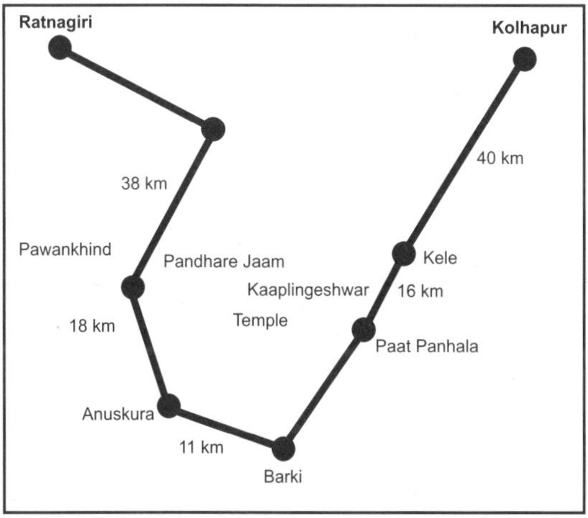

BARKI WATERFALLS

5. Gudhe Panchgani

The peripheries of Shirala taluka located in the lap of the Western Ghaats to the west of Sangli district directly merge into the districts of Ratnagiri, Kolhapur and Satara. Blessed with abundant natural beauty and comprising of many mountains, valleys and rivers, Shirala attracts tourists for various reasons. It is to this Battis Shirala that tourists from all over the world flock to witness the Naag-Panchmi celebrations wherein poisonous snakes are deftly handled by snake-charmers and later carried in processions around the village.

Places like the dam of Chandoli, the national sanctuary of Ukhlu, the famous waterfall of Dhavlewadi and the wide plateaus of Bambarwadi and Gudhe Panchgani are attracting many tourists. The way to Gudhe Panchgani goes over small and big waterfalls, streams and the waterfront of Chandoli's dam. The famous Kandhar waterfall is also here.

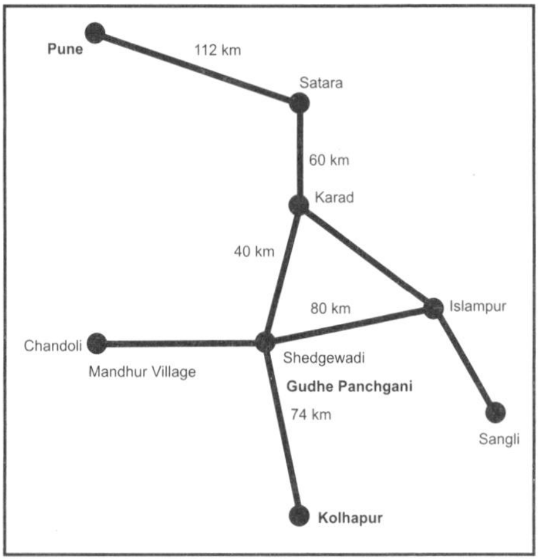

It is amazing to see the hundreds of windmills erected here by Maharashtra Urja Vikas Abhikaran (Mahaurja) to generate electricity, taking advantage of the winds blowing in from the sea at Ratnagiri over the plateaus here. While there are no arrangements for lodging at Gudhe Panchgani, there are good hotels at Shedgewadi, Charan and Warnavati.

The office and rest house of The Chandoli National Sanctuary are located at Warnavati. The officers and staff at these places are always ready to guide tourists.

Distance: Chandoli

(Satara district) - Via Karad-Shedgewadi route, Chandoli is 55 km
(Kolhapur district) – Via Kolhapur-Shedgewadi route, Chandoli is 60 km
(Sangli district) – Via Islampur-Shedgewadi route, Chandoli is 80 km
Phone nos. (02345) 226248/226318/271986
Kasav Naala, Kandahar waterfall, Kolamviche Pathar at Nivle

Distance from Karad (to Gudhe Panchgani) is 40 km; from Kolhapur is 74 km; from Islampur is 44 km

6. Ramtirtha

While going from Gadhinglaj to Amboli, one comes across a river running amidst the greenery. Her name is Hiranyakeshi. The century-old bridge on this river was named by the British as Victoria Jubilee Bridge. One can visit the temple cluster of Ramtirtha located close to this river. At one point, the river water falls from a small height to make a little waterfall. While the waterfall is not very high, it is a good spot for a one-day family picnic. The banks of Hiranyakeshi are covered with dense foliage. The azure skies above and the accompanying serenity creates a wonderful combination. The waterfall emanates a soothing melody that further fills the heart with joy. The surroundings of Ramtirtha captivate one beyond belief.

The sanctum sanctorum of the Ram Mandir contains small idols of Rampanchayatan. There's also a separate idol of Shri Hanuman. On coming out of the Ram Mandir and climbing a flight of stairs, one sees a stone-carved temple. The exquisitely carved idol of Nandi, decorated with beautiful ornaments, catches the eye. The Shivlinga in the sanctum sanctorum is smaller as compared to the Nandi, but is yet impressive.

To visit the Hiranyakeshi River and the Ramtirtha cluster of temples, one needs to go via the route going towards Amboli from Gadhinglaj. The Ramtirtha temple is located 21 km from Gadhinglaj.

Distance:

Kolhapur to Gadhinglaj – 75 km, Gadhinglaj to Ramtirtha – 21 km

Travel expense (per person charges for ST bus)

Pune to Ramtirtha – Rs 240, Mumbai to Ramtirtha – Rs 460, Nagpur to Ramtirtha – Rs 740

Arrangements for lodging and eating: Ramtirtha is a holy place located away from the town, near the river. Obviously, there's no arrangement for lodging and eating over here. One can carry tiffin to enjoy a nice lunch in the jungle. Gadhinglaj has good hotels for lodging. Other details about lodging are same as Saamangad.

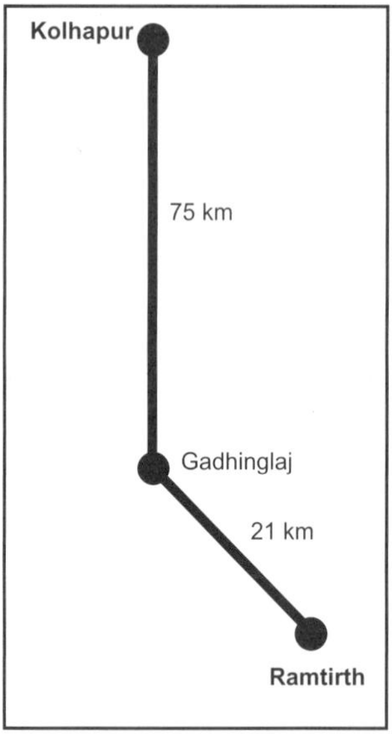

Ramtirth

Daityasoodan Temple at Lonar

Sunser at Lonar Lake

Temple priests at Nashik

Naneghat

Purandar Fort

7. Saamangad

Beyond Kolhapur, near the peak of the ghaat near the Gadhinglaj village lies a unique mountain that combines the greenery of Konkan and the cool atmosphere of the ghaats. Most of the construction on this mountain has been done below the earth (!) and it is said that from an aerial view one can see the mountain looking like the religious symbol Om (or Aum)! Saamangad is located on this mountain. The mountain contains the remains of a fort and a temple on either side.

The temple is in an area called Ramkhadi (in Saamangad). In front of the main temple is a courtyard constructed in cement. A small tortoise made of marble is installed in front of the sanctum sanctorum. The idol of Shri Hanuman in the sanctum sanctorum is south-facing and has a captivating divine expression. Surprisingly, one does not see sindoor (orange fragrant paste) smeared on this idol as it is usually on idols of Shri Hanuman.

Outside the temple, there's an ancient cave with a very narrow entrance.

From Saamnagad, one can view the nearby forts and the emerald beauty of Amboli.

Towards the right side of the temple, one can see an old house (wada) built from within the earth's surface. Though there are no records about when this wada was built, from the architecture one surmises it must be almost a thousand years old. You can go down into the wada climbing down a staircase made of purple stone.

The Shivlinga has a mask made of brass. When the mask and ornaments are removed, then only can one see the actual linga. The idol of the hooded snake standing atop the linga is also beautiful.

There's a cave towards one side of the wada. Most of the caves here are east-facing so that the rays of the rising sun first fall upon the meditating person.

Apart from small caves, one also sees a big agnikund (a special metal contraption created to pour oblations into the fire). Centuries back saints and pirs residing here must have used such agnikunds for their yagnas (sacrificial ritual). One of the caves inside the fort is very huge from within, though it has a very narrow entrance.

Devotees have installed a Shri Datta temple in one of the caves whereas a granary has been named Lakshmankuti. While the chronological details of the fort are a mystery, this was indeed an important location during Chhatrapati Shivaji's reign. From this fort,

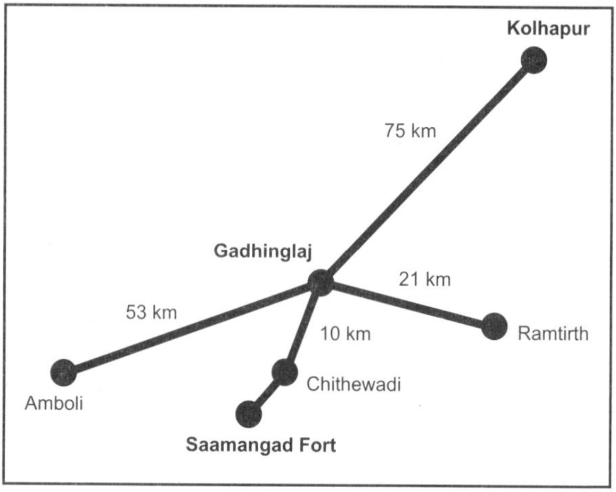

Underground Construction

weapons, ammunition and food were supplied to seven neighbouring forts such as Vallabhgad, Machchindragad, Raangna, Mahipalgad, Gandharvagad etc. Thus the name of this fort came to be Saamangad (fort of supplies!) It would be easy to store these things deep in the earth, away from the enemy's eye.

Spread over an area of 10 sq. km, this fort is faced by two hillocks, standing side by side. The sun's journey from Dakshinayan to Uttarayan (sun travelling from southern to northern hemisphere) is witnessed between these two hills – or so it is said. If you shout from the fort, its echo is heard from the opposite hills. After seeing the ancient wada and cave in this part of the fort, I went to the other end of the fort, driving through pathways hidden in dense foliage – a thrilling experience indeed. Over here too, one has to go down narrow winding steps into the earth, wondering about what surprises lay in store. The way is narrow and flanked by walls cut out from purple stone. The staircase is carved out of stone and was wet due to recent rains; thus one has to manoeuvre the way very carefully. After climbing further down and entering through a stone archway to turn right, I was stunned to see water! It was then that I realised that it was a superbly designed well.

Near this seven-arch well, is a temple erected in a shed. In it is a stone idol of Ashtabhuja Devi (eight-limbed goddess). The goddess, in her nauwari (nine-yard) attire, is around 200-300 years old. The jail here is quite spacious. It has stone benches for the prisoners to sleep on.

The remains of the fortress of Saamangad are quite extensive. At some places, trees have taken root in the walls of the fortress. Saamangad, carved out of a single block of purple stone below the earth, is waiting for the spotlight to fall on its enigmatic history. The ancient fort near Gadhinglaj is waiting for tourists and researchers.

To see the wonders of Saamangad, one should first go to Gadhinglaj near Kolhapur. Kolhapur to Gadhinglaj is 75 km whereas the fort is 9 km from Gadhinglaj. The ST bus fare for one person is Rs 240 from Pune to Saamangad; Rs 460 from Mumbai to Saamangad and Rs 740 from Nagpur to Saamangad.

Lodging and food: Gadhinglaj is a fairly large town and thus has good hotels for eating. There are small lodges and also big hotels here. Average per day tariffs range from Rs 150 to Rs 800.

8. Shri Kshetra Sitabai

Shri Sitamai/Sitabai is located at the western end of Maan taluka on a mountain peak. Towards its north begins the Phaltan taluka. Towards the west begins the periphery of Khatav taluka. To reach here, there's a 3 km long kutcha road (non-concretised road) from Kulkajai. Kulkajai is on Dahivadi-Budh route. All types of vehicles can ply on this road. However, in the monsoons it gets difficult to take vehicles due to the slush. From Phaltan, via the Veloshi route, the distance is just 27 km. However, the construction of the Veloshi ghaat road has been lying incomplete since 1987. So, vehicular movement is not possible via this road. There's a tar road from Phaltan via Tathavda going up to Budh, Rajapur and Kulkajai. The distance from Phaltan to Sitamai is 54 km.

This place is shown on the maps as 'Sitabaicha dongar' (Sitabai's mountain). The rivers Banganga and Manganga originate here. Devotees believe that Goddess Sita was staying here when expecting her twins and Luv and Kush were born here. Every year, on the day after Hanuman Jayanti i.e. Chaitra Vadya Pratipada, begins a week-long celebration that ends on Chaitra Vadya Saptami at 12 noon with the birth-celebration of Luv and Kush. All the villagers of Sathe, Taluka Phaltan donate food on this day.

Every no-moon night (Amavasya night) there's a bhajan, keertan and annadaan (singing of the Lord's praises followed by donating food) at this place. For this, twelve villages have distributed twelve months amongst themselves. Maan taluka – Kulkajai, Khokde, Kalaskarwadi,Gaadewadi, Shripaalwan; Phaltan taluka – Sathe, Takalvade, Kambleshwar, Vadle; area of Taavdi-Maalvadi-Banganga dam, Daryachi vadi and Baramati village of Baramati taluka are the twelve villages that participate.

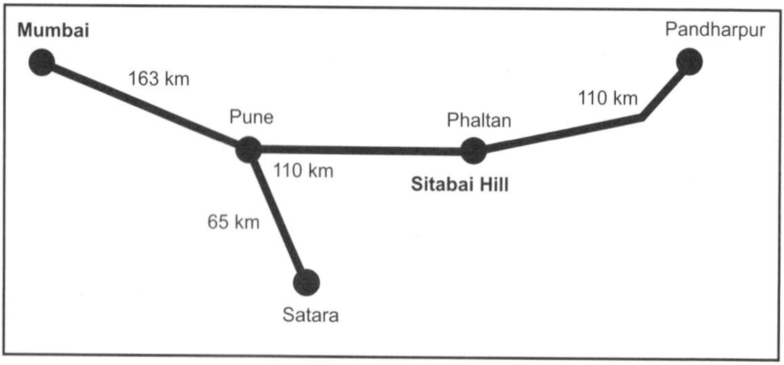

Here there's a dharamshala (dormitory) containing 38 units; that's the only place of lodging available here. There's no village or people living here. Close by, is a temple of Khandoba. Four houses belong to Waghoba and one house belongs to the priest Jagdale. Two kilometres further, is the Kalaskarvadi whose residents celebrate the week-long festival in Chaitra.

Makar Sankranti is a widely celebrated festival here and it is estimated that close to 2 lakh women come here during that time. The only facility available here is of drinking water! During festive period, temporary stalls and hotels get erected. Pilgrims congregate here during Aashadhi Amavasya. As per our sources, this is the only village in Maharashtra that celebrates the birth of Luv-Kush and that too with a week-long fest! If the route from Phaltan via Veloshi ghaat is constructed properly to enable ST buses to ply on it, this temple will flourish all the more. This scenic and historically-important place has stayed away from the limelight due to lack of proper transportation resources. Shri Sitamai Devasthan Trust, Kulkajai, oversees the affairs of this temple. The air and water here are totally pollution-free.

If transportation begins via Veloshi ghaat, the neighbouring 30-35 villages will get connected to Shri Sitamai; thus increasing the prosperity of all these places.

For more details, contact:
Shri Jyotiram Dhembre, Phaltan
Phone (02166-223513)

Distance: Phaltan to Pune 110 km; Phaltan to Satara – 65 km; Phaltan to Pandharpur – 110 km

Sitabai Hill

9. Shikhar-Shingnapur

There are two important religious places in Maharashtra – Shani Shingnapur and Shikhar Shingnapur. I had already been to Shani Shingnapur – the place near Nasik-Shirdi famous for its houses having no doors. It is also famous for its folklore that says that any person stealing anything will immediately die by vomiting blood! I was now curious to see Shikhar Shingnapur – due to the similarity of its name with Shani Shingnapur and its history connected with Chhatrapati's Shivaji's reign. My wish got fulfilled whilst shooting for a regional Marathi film 'Shambhu Majha Navsacha' at Shikhar Shingnapur. I acted in this film along with Alka Kubal, Prasad Oak, Teja Devkar, Nagesh Bhosle, etc.

Shikhar Shingnapur is 36 km away from Phaltan. Pune-Phaltan is a 2 hour long stretch; the time will probably be reduced after the tunnel of Katraj is constructed. It stands at an altitude of 2900 ft from sea-level – approximately as high as Raigad. Known as Kothalgiri, this mountain comes in the Mann taluka of Satara district. In 1589, Malojiraje Bhosle, the grandfather of Chhatrapati Shivaji, had also built a water tank called Pushkartirth, at this place. Originally built in the Chalukya style of architecture, the temple was renovated, restored and re-consecrated by the Chhatrapati himself, as records prove. The Chhatrapati used to reside in the mansion opposite the temple. Its ownership, along with the ownership of the temple, still lies with the Bhosles of Satara, heirs of the Chhatrapati. The task of welcoming Netaji Palkar back into Hinduism happened in front of the Chhatrapati himself, at this very spot – or so it is said.

There's a concrete road leading directly to the main door of the temple. But you can also climb up the steps from the village. One encounters the Pushkartirth tank and a Ganesh temple on the way. Then comes a huge arch, called Shendge Darwaza and then an area called Jijamata Ves. There's an idol of Lord Saturn installed here. Further ahead are the idols of Lord Shiva, Hanuman and Ganesh. After this, we enter the courtyard of the temple. The originally-stone temple has now been painted pink. Therefore, it looks like the temples found in South India. One can see a unique thing here – two Shivalings and five Nandis!

---

*(*kavadis: two pails hanging on either sides of a wooden rod; used for carrying water on the shoulders).*

One can also come here via Mungi ghaat. Every year during the Chaitra month fair, around 400-500 people come here via the Mungi ghaat to fulfil their promises to the Lord, carrying kavadis* for the same. They bathe the Shivaling with water – the scene is worth seeing.

Guptlinga, a spot that is 3 km away from the ST stand, is also worth a visit. There are eight lingas (apart from the main Guptlinga) that stand surrounding Lord Shambhu Mahadev here. These are known as Eklinga, Paanlinga, Khamlinga, Umbardev, Gourihar, Beldev, Vaildev etc. Due to the presence of all these lingas, Shikhar Shingnapur is also known as Dakshin Kailash.

There's a government rest-house at the foothills. Good food is available in the village. The surroundings of the rest-house look quite good due to the huge trees and the imposing mountain standing behind, but insect pests are a problem. Therefore, it is better to stay at Phaltan, see Shikhar Shingnapur during the day and return by night.

SHIKHAR SHINGNAPUR TEMPLE

10. The Mystery of Kaalbhairav

However technologically and scientifically advanced our society may become, some phenomena still remain an enigma. Maybe a few years down the line, their secrets might be revealed but till then, the mystery continues....! I'm presenting before you one such mysterious story narrated by a friend Nitin Abhyankar, which has especially remained in my memory.

We all are familiar with the famous town renowned for the Mahalakshmi temple - Karvir Nagari aka Kolhapur. Around 60 km away from this town, is Gadhinglaj. There are many hotels in Gadhinglaj, which is also a big market place for Sankeshwari chillies. There are nice temples of Nanjaya, Mahadev, Hanuman, Vitthal and Lakshmi in this village. On the day of Dussehra, palanquins of the respective Gods set out from these temples. Amidst the beat of drums and the tinkle of cymbals, the palanquins come to the village periphery to cross over it. From there on, there ensues a race between these palanquins that whizzes forward through farms and forests to reach the Nanjaya temple. Normally, the palanquin of Shri Hanuman reaches first. The palanquins are bathed in the water of the Hiranyakeshi River, situated close to the Nanjaya temple after which they're brought back to their respective temples.

As we move away from Gadhinglaj towards Nipani via the Bahirewadi route, 4 km down is the Kaalbhairav temple connected to our story.

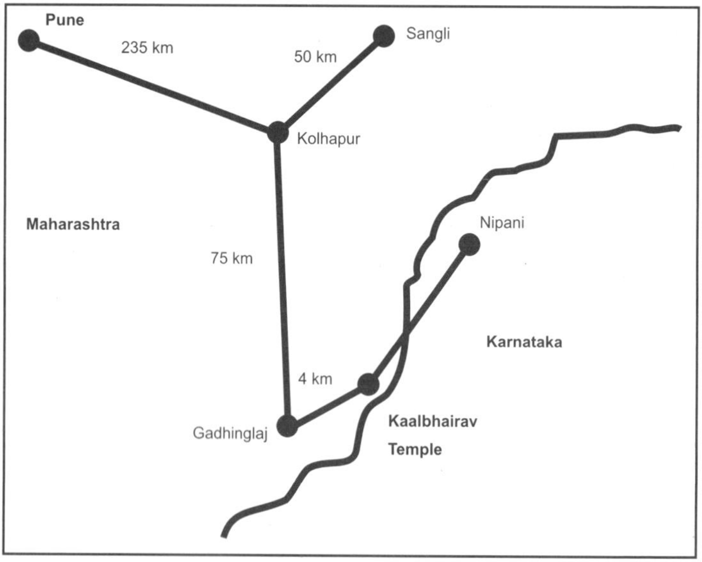

This temple built during the reign of Pandavas, is on the Shendri Mountain. Climbing approximately 300 steps, we reach the temple. The non-concretised road also takes us to the temple. This spot is on the Maharashtra-Karnataka border. Every Sunday, there's a huge crowd of devotees over here. Similarly, on each no-moon night (amavasya) there's a ritual to flay a stick around the premises and many devotees come to offer coconuts.

Near the Kaalbhairav temple, there's a freshwater spring that flows perennially. Devotees who ask for a boon, come all the way from Gadhinglaj, walking, making a saashtang namaskar by touching the entire body to the ground and then again walking before repeating this ritual all over again! Only after taking a dip in this freshwater spring is the boon considered granted and thanked for.

Each year, during Chaitra Purnima (full-moon night in the month of Chaitra), there's a huge fest at the Kaalbhairav temple. On the preceding day, villagers feast on puranpoli (a sweet delicacy made of besan, sugar and maida) and gather near the temple.

On the day of the fest, devotees flocking from all over Maharashtra and Karnataka sacrifice thousands of goats. However, the meat is not taken into the main temple. The slit heads of the goats are neatly aligned near the stone idol of Tolbhairav, installed just outside the temple.

On that night, no one stays at the temple. All the devotees and the priest step down to stay in the village.

However, when one reaches near the Tolbhairav's idol in the morning, there is absolutely no trace of any goat-head! Neither is there a drop of blood on the ground! The area around the temple is not thickly forested. There's not a single wild beast that can eat so many goat-heads in one night. That so many goat-heads vanish without a trace in one night is nothing less than a miracle!

A thoroughly scientific and practical man like Nitin too has no choice but to believe that it is indeed a miracle.

NORTH KONKAN, DAMAN & DIU

1. Sanjan's Walking Tree & Daman

In the north of Mumbai, i.e. in North Konkan, there are many places to visit – especially unknown forts and lesser-known coastal strips. Bordi-Dahanu, Narpad, Naargil, Kelwe-Mahim are some of these coastal strips that have stayed away from limelight. Along with them are mountain peaks such as Tungareshwar, Takmak, Tandulwadi, Asherigad and Kohoj. All of these contain dense forests and strong forts. There are also some famous tourist spots such as Silvassa, Khanvel, Daman and Sanjan. Although Sanjan is not a part of Maharashtra and Daman and Silvassa are Union Territories, since these are located on the border of Maharashtra, one can see an inter-mingling of cultures happening here. There are beautiful ponds, huge orchards and small sanctuaries with exotic animals. A speciality of this area are the dense chikoo orchards that allow no sunlight to pass through them!

I was quite curious about Sanjan in Gujarat because I had heard about a 'walking mango tree' located here! I had read an article about it and was curious to see for myself. I happened to be in Khanvel for a shoot and when I got a day off, decided to check out Sanjan and its walking tree for myself!

Eighty-eight kilometres from Bandra in Mumbai, on the Mumbai-Ahmedabad highway, is Manor. Bandra to Talasari, the distance is 132 km. From Talasari, one road branches out towards Umbargaon. This road also goes to Sanjan, which is 16 km from Talsari.

On reaching Sanjan, what attracts your attention, is the pillar belonging to the Parsi community. When the Parsis first entered India a few centuries ago, they settled at Sanjan – this pillar is a memorial for the same. Thus it is also called the Parsi Memorial. Technically, it is called The Memorial Pillar of Sanjan. Names of some of the Parsi people who came at that time and stayed at Sanjan, are carved on this pillar. I observed this pillar and clicked a few snaps. There's a beautiful garden created around this pillar and at the back of this garden is a house. I wanted to find out where exactly is the walking tree located and thus went into the house to enquire. There I met a teacher called Mr Davne who volunteered to show me the tree.

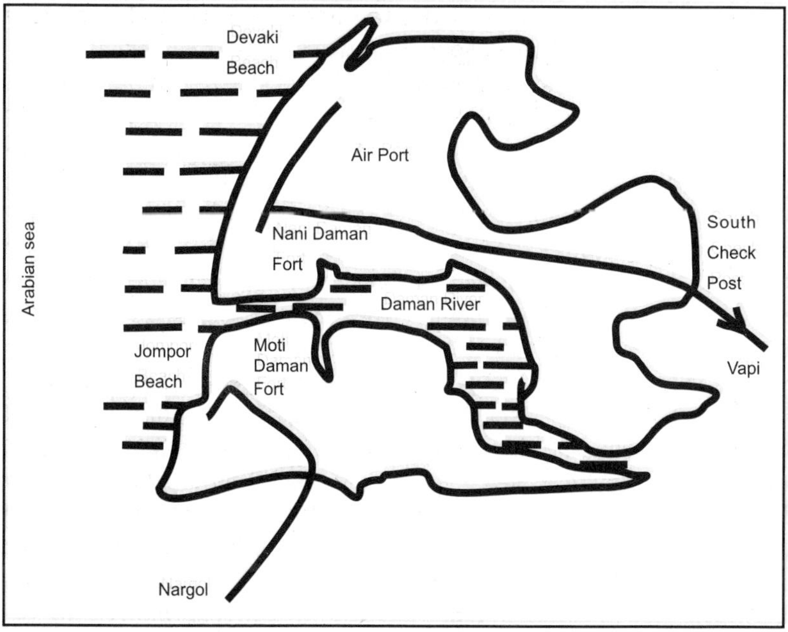

Sunset at Daman

The tree was located 2-3 km away from the pillar and in a place owned by a Parsi family called Diviyerwala. The Diviyerwalas' house was a typical old-world Parsi structure that we see in Mumbai at places like Nariman Point, Fountain or Malabar Hill. An entirely wooden structure, it had glass windows set in wooden frames and had teak-wood staircases created in a typically Parsi fashion. The house was decorated also in a very typically Parsi way and contained things like a box for paan (betel leaf) and betelnut, animal figurines, porcelain vessels etc. It becomes evident that one is getting the pleasure of seeing an authentic Parsi household, made especially so due to the photographs and paintings of a very revered saint of the sect. Later, when the family members of the Diviyerwala family posed for pictures, one could witness a Parsi family exactly as one envisions it, to be standing in front of you. These people were so helpful, that when I expressed a desire to see the walking tree, their son and daughter themselves came along to show it. They had heard about me writing travel-features. Hence, they themselves offered some old documents they had, to refer to if I wanted to write about Sanjan and its walking tree! The documents contained detailed information about how the Parsis came to Sanjan and also about the walking tree.

This walking tree is located 3 km from Sanjan, on a farm and is surrounded by palm and coconut trees. The walking tree is located a furlong away, at the other end of the farm. I met some old farmers and adivasis, who told me that their ancestors had seen the tree coming right up to the middle of the farm! We also saw this tree having moved quite a bit ahead from its point of origin. This tree is such that it grows very close to the earth. One side of the tree is bent with its branches coming out. These branches then penetrate into the earth and take the earth's support as the roots do. Thus, the tree breaks off from where it had earlier begun and makes a new beginning from where the branches erupt again from the ground. Thus, in this way, the tree moves a few metres in a couple of years. There are many proofs to support this fact, which is also reaffirmed by many villagers who've seen this phenomenon over the years. Mr Diviyerwala's daughter told us that now, since the tree is going outside their compound, they are toying with the idea of buying the plot beyond their present one! Mr Diviyerwala's daughter Parichher and son Ardeshir, also told me that this tree is 1200 years old and moves 1 yard each year. They've tried grafting this tree and re-locating it but the efforts have not borne much fruit. The tree bears fruit which resembles the usual mango but is a bit more tapering and oval. People are ready to purchase one mango for as high as Rs 25, due to the faith associated with it!

Koyna Forest Reserve

Original painting of Mastani
Nana Phadnavis Wada

Fishing boats outside
Vijayadurg fort

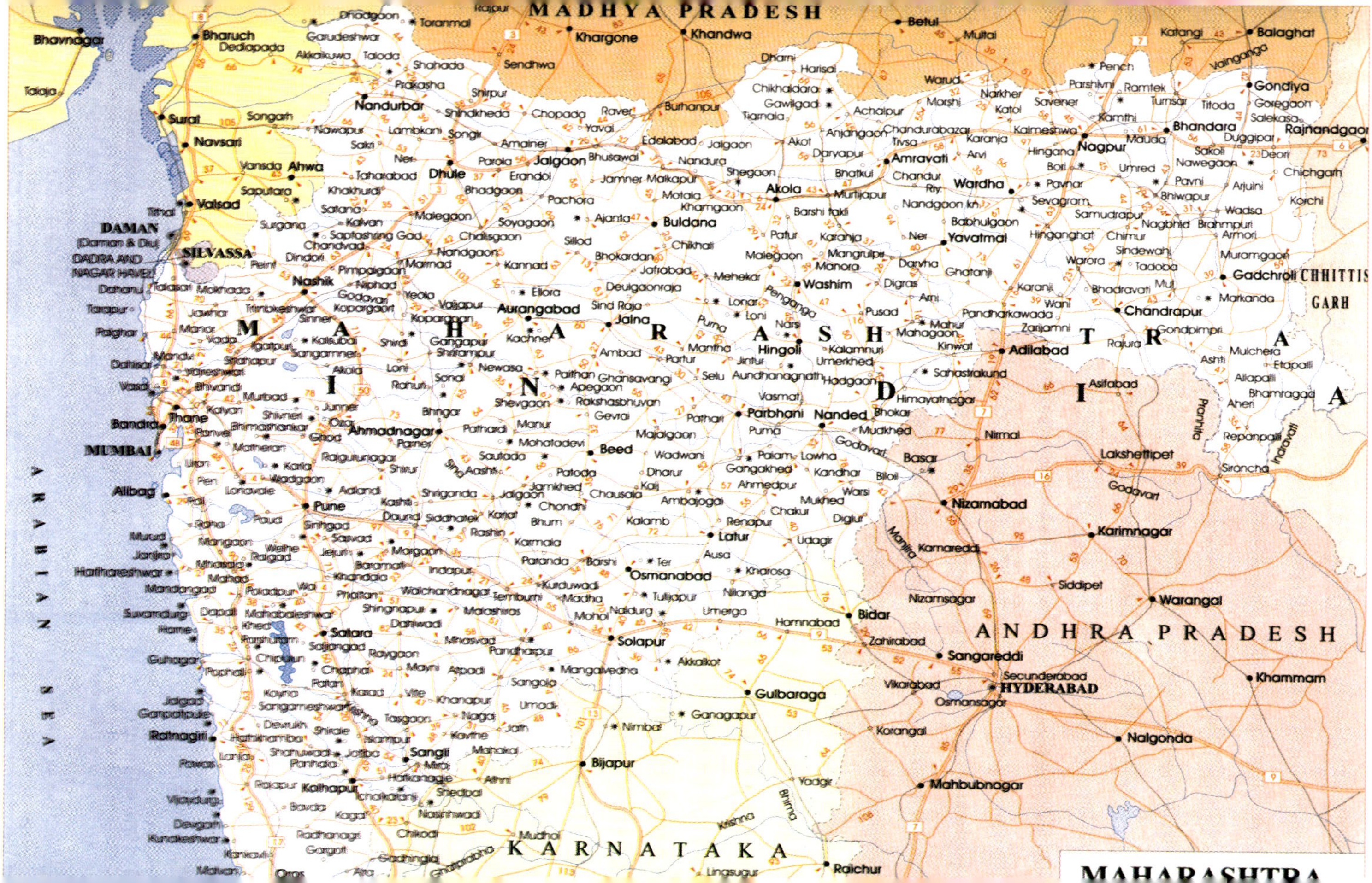
MAHARASHTRA
MADHYA PRADESH
ANDHRA PRADESH
KARNATAKA
CHHITTIS GARH
ARABIAN SEA
DAMAN (Daman & Diu)
DADRA AND NAGAR HAVELI
SILVASSA
MUMBAI
Thane
Bandra
Alibag
Pune
Nashik
Dhule
Nandurbar
Jalgaon
Aurangabad
Ahmadnagar
Beed
Jalna
Buldana
Akola
Amravati
Washim
Hingoli
Parbhani
Nanded
Latur
Osmanabad
Solapur
Satara
Sangli
Kolhapur
Ratnagiri
Yavatmal
Wardha
Nagpur
Bhandara
Gondiya
Gadchiroli
Chandrapur
Bharuch
Surat
Navsari
Valsad
Bhavnagar
Khargone
Khandwa
Betul
Balaghat
Rajnandgaon
Adilabad
Nizamabad
Karimnagar
Warangal
Sangareddi
HYDERABAD
Secunderabad
Khammam
Nalgonda
Mahbubnagar
Bidar
Gulbarga
Bijapur
Raichur

Walking tree of Sanjan

The Diviyerwalas, A Typical Parsi Family

From the Diviyerwalas and the documents they had, I got much information about the history of the Parsis who settled here. In the 7th century, to escape from the clutches of the fanatic Arab tormentors, almost 2000 Zoroastrians set sail in a boat from Iran and as luck would have it, got caught in a sea storm near Diu. To remain safe in the storm, they prayed that they would erect a Holy Flame of Fire (their place of worship) when they reached Hindusthan. Amongst them, was a great spiritual leader and astrologer called Dastur. He predicted that they would be safe if they managed to reach Hindusthan. The boat somehow reached Diu and then Sanjan. Sanjan was the ruled by a kind king called Jadi Rana. He gave solace to the distraught Parsis. The Parsis expressed a desire to stay at Sanjan – a wish that the benign Jadi Rana granted and thus the Parsis came to settle in India. Jadi Rana was said to be a descendant of the Shilaharas. We can also see Jadi Rana's fort at Sanjan; as also the spot where the Parsis landed (which is seen from the fort).

After seeing Sanjan, its walking tree and the fort, proceed 11 km ahead to the exquisite beach of Nargol. One can see a small island made of sand, in the sea at Nargol. The fisherfolk stay on this island. One can see numerous wooden poles erected in the sand with fish hung to dry over them. A photographer can capture a breathtaking view of the sunset in the backdrop of these poles.

From Nargol, one can travel 24 km to reach Daman. If you want to stay at Sanjan, there are some good hotels. Globe Hotel is one of them. Here, the room charges range from Rs.350 to Rs.600. Tel nos: 02602345243.

However, it is more convenient to stay at Daman.

Daman is 24 km away from Sanjan and is divided into two parts: Moti Daman and Nani Daman.

The Damanganga River has created these two parts out of the 72 sq.km area. We can come to the Jampor beach in Moti Daman, from Nargol. Another way to come to Moti or Nani Daman is to come via the Mumbai-Ahmedabad highway and turn left from Vapi. Ten kilometres ahead of the turn, is Daman. Daman is 192 km from Mumbai. It is convenient to come from Vapi to Daman from the Mumbai-Ahmedabad expressway. The coast of Moti Daman is called Jampor beach. The beach is flanked by beautiful, swaying casuarina trees. The sunset here is a must-see. The Daman Nagar Tourist Complex contains cottages to stay, avenues for water sports etc.

Like Goa, Daman too was ruled by the Portuguese. We can see their fort – the Fort of Moti Daman. It is pentagonal fort spread over approx. 30,000 sq. m. The Portuguese tried to seize this fort from the Sultan of Gujarat from 1523. Finally, they became successful in 1559. One can see signs of Portuguese lifestyle in the fort. The fort has 10 bastions and 2 doors. It also has buildings such as the Governor's palace, Collectorate, Secretariat etc.

Nani Daman too has a fort called St. Jerome Fort. This fort was built to protect Daman from the Mughal invasion from 1614 to 1627. This fort has 3 bastions with a door near each bastion. Amongst these doors, the one facing the river has beautiful sculptures of St. Jerome and two other men.

Presently, the fort houses a school and a Christian cemetery. Just as Moti Daman has the Jampor beach, Nani Daman has the amazing Devka beach. This beach is also flanked by casuarina trees. The beach is located 5 km to the north of Nani Daman. It is dangerous to swim in this beach since it has a rocky bed. Nearby, there are amusement parks and restaurants serving various cuisines. The lighthouse here is also worth seeing. Apart from this, in Daman, the Cathedral of Bom Jesus (a wood 'n brick church built in 1603), Church of Our Lady and the Dominical Monastery are also worth seeing. The Satyasagar Garden is also nice for a visit.

Like Goa, one can also find Indian and imported liquor at dirt-cheap rates, at Daman. Thus, there are numerous wine shops to be spotted here.

One can stay at hotels charging anything between Rs 150 to Rs 2000. Some of these are: Hotel Ashoka Palace, tel. no. 0260 – 2254993; China Town, tel. no. 0260 – 2254420; Jazira, tel. no. 0260 – 2254330; Government Rest House, tel. no. 0260 – 2255032.

2. Silvassa and Khanvel

From childhood, I was quite intrigued about Daman & Diu and Dadra & Nagar Haveli – names I had till then encountered only on maps. Firstly, the names sounded quite unique; then, these places were standing by themselves, without being a part of any state; and, thus, because they were controlled directly by the Union Government, they were called Union Territories. All these facts were enough to spark a curiosity in my little mind at that time. I was curious about how these UTs looked, what their inmates did, and whether there were any forests, mountains and valleys or animals. Later in life, when I toured Vikramgad, Jawahar, and Wada, I first saw Khanvel. That was when the Saakartod River was flowing with abundant water. Recently, I happened to visit Khanvel and Silvassa due to my shooting sojourns.

Coming into this area, one feels delighted on seeing red acacia and gulmohur trees flanking the tar road, which inevitably gets decorated by the flowers raining down on it all day long.

A cluster of approximately 72 villages, this region was ruled by the Portuguese for almost 150 years. The area of this region is 491 sq. km.

In Portuguese, Silva means trees or jungle. Silvassa was thus named due to its dense foliage. There's a garden called 'Hirva Van' on the Dadra-Silvassa road. Miniature waterfalls, well-manicured lawns of lush green grass and flowering trees make it an ideal garden – one that enhances Silvassa's beauty all the more. There is another beautiful garden called 'Vaanganga Lake Garden' 5 km from Silvassa, which is the capital of Dadra. Quite a few Bollywood movies are shot here due to the scenic beauty. Yet another such beautiful garden is located 20 km from Silvassa, near Khanvel. It is called 'Vanvihar Tourist Complex'. Well-manicured lawns, small hillocks, a cactus-park containing various specimens of cactii and a deer-park make this place look inviting. These gardens remind you of Ooty's Botanical Garden or Goregaon's Chhota Kashmir.

Dudhni is 20 km from Khanvel. Here, one can see the backwaters of Madhuban dam located on Damanganga River. One can stay in tents erected close to the river.

Apart from this, Our Lady of Pity Church, located on Naroli Road, gives a glimpse into the Portuguese era in its architecture.

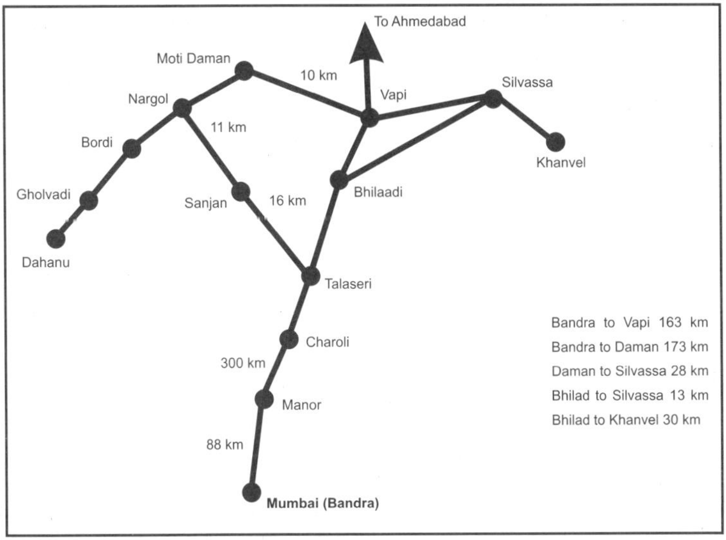

SILVASSA DEER PARK

At Vasona near Silvassa, three lions have been brought from Gir Sanctuary, to create a lion park. This small sanctuary spread over an area of 20 hectares, is fenced in with barbed wire. Inside, there are roads almost 2.6 km long. Safely ensconced in vehicles fitted with nets, one can see the lions roaming around in the sanctuary.

I was curious about how these UTs looked, what their inmates did, and whether there were any forests, mountains and valleys or animals.

Another place worth seeing in Silvassa is the Saatmajiya Deer Park. The park is located to the south of Silvassa, 12 km down the Silvassa-Khanvel road. It is spread over 300 hectares and one can see animals like saambar (stag), neelgai (blue bull), chital (spotted deer) and choushinga (four horned antelope). The Taadkeshwar Mahadev temple and the Adivasi museum are also worth seeing.

Silvassa has good hotels such as Raas Resort, Hotel Ritz, Woodland and Green Wood; while Khanvel has the Khanvel resort. The ambience is beautiful and one gets amazing veg and non-veg food.

Tel nos. 02602677401/02103

Mumbai – 02226207966/26289370

The Pink Rose hotel and Sakarvan hotel are also good.

LONAVLA/KHANDALA KARJAT/MURBAD

1. Umbarkhind

The Diwekars of Vikramgad, who I've mentioned in my first book 'Majhi Mulukhgiri', have a 35-acre farmhouse at Doorshet on the Pali-Khopoli road, which has also become quite famous. Their son Chinmay looks into the project himself. I've included information about Doorshet in the second book of Bhatkanti. Chinmay and his father have developed a lot of tourist spots in and around Doorshet. These include places like Thanale, Khadsamble Leni, Paalicha Ganpati, Uddhar Rameshwar, Sarasgad, the hot springs at Unhere, Umbarkhind and such other little-known or totally unknown places. Amongst these, Umbarkhind is an important location in the historical sense; especially for those wanting to make a detailed study of the guerrilla warfare that Chhatrapati Shivaji deployed to defeat the huge Mughal army. Half an hour from Doorshet by the coast of Amba river, one can see Umbarkhind at the foot of the well-known points of Lonavla, including Duke's Nose, Nagfani or INS Shivaji.

In 1661 AD, the Mughal general and Aurangzeb's uncle Shaista Khan employed the Uzbek warrior Kaartab Khan and the Rajput woman Raibaaghan (later called as Ranragini) to catch Chhatrapati Shivaji. On 2nd February 1661, Khan was descending upon Konkan via the Pali-Khopoli route with an army of 30,000 Mughal warriors. The Chhatrapati was watching his actions with a keen eye. When the army reached a very narrow strip of Umbarkhind, Chhatrapati's army swooped down to trap them there and soon, the huge Mughal army was badly defeated by the handful of Marathas! Raibaaghan was later sent back with due respects. Kaartab Khan's humiliation and the Marathas' joyous victory is an unforgettable memory attached to Umbarkhind's history – thus making it an important place. On coming to this place, one can easily make out how the Marathas must have skilfully trapped the Mughal army and defeated it.

It is convenient to stay at Doorshet and come visiting here. On the Pali-Khopoli route, Doorshet is located 85 km from Sion and 100 km from Pune.

Doorshet to Umbarkhind, the distance is a mere 4 km.

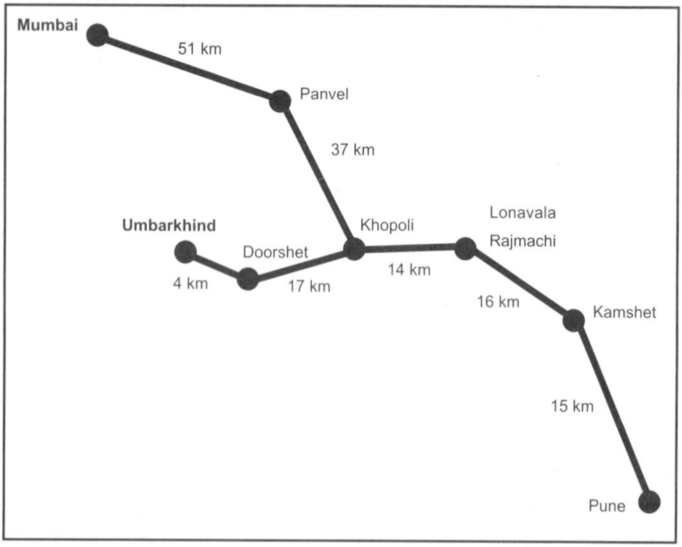

THANALE CAVES

2. Visawa Resort

A resort that does complete justice to its name, Visawa resort is located 44 km on the Kalyan-Nagar route, on the banks of a small river called Doifodi near Saralgaon

In keeping with their hobby of creating rose plantations, Drs Vijay and Meghna Mhaskar had developed a huge 12-acre 'Meghna Farm' at Kalyan even as they took care of their hospital. Today it is called the Visawa resort. Steeped in the loving toil of 13-14 years, the resort is now a haven for innumerable tourists. The Mhaskars converted their private farm into a resort with an aim to let other nature-loving people enjoy some natural beauty in a city that is otherwise a concrete jungle! The name Visawa (a secluded haven) welcomes people who want to rest and rejuvenate their stressed body mind in the midst of serene nature.

Matheran, Mahaleshwar and such picnic spots are quite far away from Mumbai. It is quite time-consuming to travel to and from these places. In comparison, Visawa resort is quite convenient a choice due to being within 100 km from Mumbai and due to the smooth approach roads that make travelling hassle-free. One can go to Visawa Resort via the Eastern Express Highway from Mumbai to Kalyan and from Kalyan to Saralgaon through the Nagar road. 30 km from Kalyan, you'll come to Murbad and 12 km from there comes Saralgaon. Taking a left from Saralgoan, 2 km on the Kinavhli road, you reach Visawa resort.

If you don't have a vehicle, then catch any bus that goes via Malshej ghaat from the bus-stand outside Kalyan station (west). Get down at Saralgaon bus-stop (which is 42 km away from Kalyan) and hire a rickshaw or jeep, which will take you directly to the resort at a charge of Rs 6 per person. From Nasik, one can

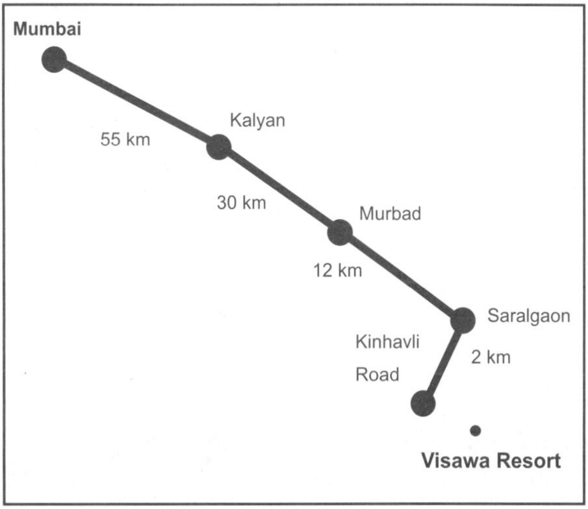

come to the resort via the Shahpur-Kinavhli route; while, from Pune one can reach the resort via Aalefata road or through the expressway (which is around 180 km from the resort).

At Visawa, there's something for everyone. There are bicycles/ tricycles for kids; many games such as cricket, badminton, volleyball, basketball, indoor games, carrom, table-tennis, chess, darts etc for grown-ups. There's also a spacious and beautiful swimming pool, an artificial waterfall as also an artificial rainfall that can be enjoyed here.

If you feel like enjoying in isolation, reading or listening to songs on a walkman, there are sit-outs created amidst dense foliage, that give you complete privacy in the lap of nature. A small but well-stocked library is available at the disposal of book-lovers; whereas those with an artistic bent of mind, have paints and paper waiting for them! Roaming idyllically through the landscaped gardens becomes all the more enjoyable in the company of poet Chandrashekhar Gokhale's 'Chaarolya' along with the greenery and floral wealth all around.

There are around 1500 rose-shrubs of around 450 species in the famous 'Babanchya Baaget' which has won numerous prizes in rose-shows all over Maharashtra. The road leading towards this garden is canopied with vines and has lotuses floating in ponds along its side, which makes the 300 m long walk, a walk in heaven!

The pillars in this walkway are etched with information about rose-plantation, history of roses and what's more, poetry about roses! The delightful fragrance of roses that wafts from afar strongly arouses a desire to create a similar, if small, rose-garden at our home too!

The international names of the roses specified here, and the weekly class (every Saturday) about rose-plantation, increases our knowledge manifold.

There's variety in the cuisines available here too. Indian vegetarian, Chinese, Jain etc are some of the types of scrumptious food that you can taste here. There's also non-vegetarian fare for those who prefer that.

After meals, women-folk can indulge in 'mehendi-drawing' (drawing patterns on hand with henna paste). Women are happy to come here because of the familial atmosphere that Visawa offers. It's a treat to take a walk on the banks of Doifodi River early in the morning or evening. Visawa also has a conference hall enough to accommodate 70-80 executives at a time – thus making it a preferred location for seminars, conferences etc. Since the resort is well-equipped with generators, there's no worry about power-cuts.

Despite offering so much, the charges at Visawa are extremely affordable. The per day rate (from morning to evening) is Rs 250 per person; whereas the cost for a 2 day-1 night package is Rs 700 per person. The rates are inclusive of vegetarian food but in case you want non-vegetarian food, then, separate rates apply. Discounts are offered for school students, senior citizens and schools for the handicapped, on all days except weekends and public holidays.

Just 5 km away from Visawa is a beautiful confluence and a temple of Lord Shiva. Lenyadri-Ozar (two amongst the Ashtavinayaks) are approximately 70-80 km way from Visawa. One can also visit the Ganpati mandir of Titwala or the Birla mandir whilst arriving or returning.

Nowadays, the entire affairs of Visawa are handled by the doctors' son Sanket and his wife Gauri.

One simply does not feel like steeping out of this secluded haven and when one does it is only with fond memories and a strong desire to return soon.

Contact: 'Visawa Resort', Mhaskar hospital, C/o, Murbad road, Kalyan (W) Thana district.

Tel nos: 9821116631/95251-2329123/2329141.

Spots to visits from Visawa:

(Given in the order of name of the place with its importance; best way to reach there; and distance from Visava)

1) Titwala Ganpati (place of worship), own vehicle, 34 km
2) Lenyadri–Ozar (Ashtavinayak), own vehicle, (via Malshej) 60-70 km
3) Birla Mandir of Shahad (place of worship), own vehicle, (Via Kalyan road) 41 km
4) Lord Shiva temple (made of marble), rickshaw/own vehicle, 5 km
5) Famous fort of Siddhagad, bus/own vehicle, 32 km
6) Naneghaat, bus/own vehicle, 20 km
7) Famous fort of Harishchandragad, bus/own vehicle, 60 km
8) Tourist spot of Malshej ghaat, bus/own vehicle, 40 km
9) Barvi dam, bus/own vehicle, 26 km

3. Water sports

'Water sports' is a fairly new thing. It is best enjoyed in natural surroundings. A few such places are as follows:

1) With the assistance of Himalayan exploration (MHE), Diwekar's Nature Trails has started water sports in Maharashtra. 2½ hours away from Mumbai and Pune in the Kundalika River of Konkan; at Mulshi river and at the foothills of the mountains on which rests the Mulshi dam. One can do three types of river rafting in one hour, in a 14 km-long river. The distance is 138 km from Mumbai and 100 km from Pune. There are good arrangements for lodging over here. The rates are Rs 1099 per person for rafting; Rs 2850 p.p for rafting and lodging (one night) Life jackets, helmets, paddles, guides etc are all provided in this rate. Sutarwadi, located 8 km from Kolad on the Mumbai-Goa expressway is the actual location of this endeavour. Bookings can be done at: Nature Trails, Hemendra Shopping centre, Gokhale Road, Naupada, Thane (W) – 400602. Tel no: 25401601 / 25423586 / 25337006
2) Tapola – in the Koyna river at Mahabaleshwar, 2659 ft high
3) Dabhosa – at the beautiful, 150 ft high waterfall near Jawahar

At both these places, adventure sports such as rappelling, river-crossing, trekking, kayaking etc are conducted. Contact Nature Trails for more details.

4. Upper Deck, Lonavala

The hill stations of Lonavala-Khandala are well-known, not just amongst Mumbaikars and Punekars, but amongst avid travellers from over the whole country. Bollywood movies and songs have immensely popularised these locations. There are many new and old hotels in these two areas. I've myself stayed in quite a few of those – including Duke's Retreat, Fariyas, Girija, Vallerina, Chandralok, Annapurna etc. So much so, that I know what scenery is visible from which window in which hotel! During holidays and vacation season, places like Lonavala, Khandala, Matheran and Mahabaleshwar get so crowded with tourists, that hotel bookings are mighty difficult to get even if you call four-five days in advance!

Last Diwali, I went through a similar experience, when 2-3 families decided to go to one of these places to relax over the weekend. But since our plan was so impromptu, we couldn't get a booking in a single hotel! Finally, we got to stay at a scenic resort, courtesy some friends in the forest department.

While travelling from Mumbai to Pune when you reach Khandala, the tall mountain that's seen on the right side is called Barometer Hill. Behind the Barometer hill lies the Duke's Nose or Naagfanicha Sulka. Towards the left is also a mountain with a tower. Behind this mountain are the hills on which stand the Rajmachi fort and Dhaak fort. The road leading to Rajmachi meanders around this mountain. At the foothills of this mountain is the Tungaarli Lake. While going from Mumbai to Pune, if you go inside the Lonavala village, take the road beside the petrol-pump that you'll see immediately towards your left as you enter Lonavala. It'll take you straight to Tungaarli Lake. This road then becomes steep as it continues ahead from the mountain's back-side. That road is quite steep and badly-constructed. Hence it becomes difficult to ply small, stocky vehicles. In the middle of this mountain is a beautiful hotel-cum-resort called Upper Deck. If you inform this hotel of your arrival, you can keep your vehicle at the foothills. The hotel sends their Scorpio car to fetch you and the luggage. While climbing uphill, one can see Srivardhan, Manranjan (the twin hilltops of Rajmachi fort) and the pristine Tungaarli Lake in the valley below!

I'd taken along a Scorpio, specially built for rough tracks. Hence I did not need to change vehicles. The pin-bends towards the end of the mountain (that reminded me of Matheran) were quite tricky and dangerous and really put my driving skills to test! The people along with me were busy admiring the scenic beauty from the windows, even as I was striving to reach us all safely to the resort. The resort's

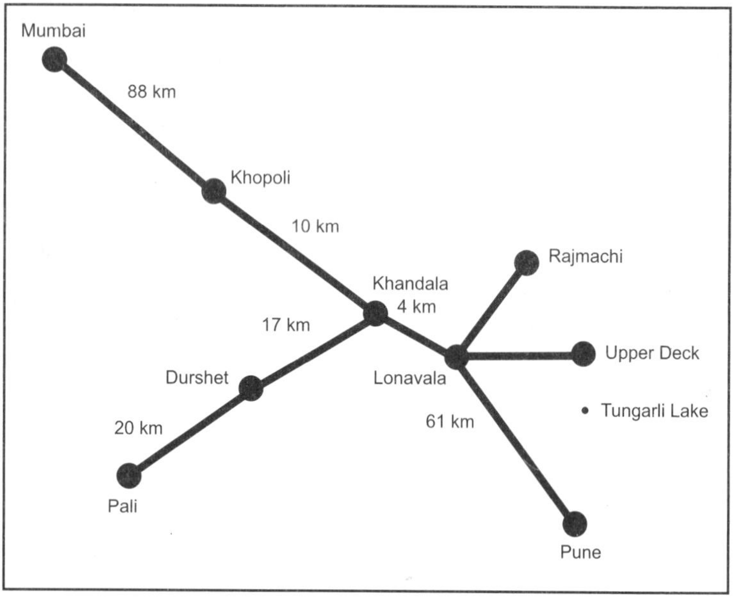

Sunset at Upper Deck Lonavala

architecture and décor; its unique location and the beauty surrounding it, fills you with praise for its creator's taste. Khandala and Lonavala are not visible from this resort, which is almost 700-800 ft high from Khandala. Thus, the resort is at an altitude of almost 2600 ft from sea-level. The neighbouring mountain standing on the other side of the valley, is equally high. It has dense forestation on its head. From the resort, one can see the pathway leading to the mountain.

This is a resort catering to the upper-middle and upper class (in terms of its charges). Thus, it has the comforts of a sauna, steam, gymnasium, meditation centre, swimming pool, Jacuzzi, six-hole golf course, badminton etc to cater to hi-fi tastes. When seen from above, the azure tone of the swimming pool in the backdrop of an equally beautiful Tungaarli lake below looks breathtaking. One can click some amazing pictures of the rising sun from this place. You can enjoy a trek up the neighbouring mountain or can also go up to the Rajmachi fort if you're willing to travel a bit farther. According to me, the two hotels that should be chosen to have a great view of the scenic beauty are Duke's Retreat and Upper Deck.

The food is also quite good at Upper Deck. Both veg and non-veg fare is served in the buffet system.

Address: Upper Deck, 13/15, Pangkholi gaon, Thakurwadi, Near Tungaarli Lake, Lonavala. Tel no.: 02114278069. Mumbai tel nos. : 22160843/5484

5. Bahiri Caves and Kundaleshwar Temple

On reaching the Saandshi village via road from Karjat, the Dhaak fort mesmerises one with its imposing beauty. Three-fourth of the way up Dhaak fort, on the steep stony plinths to its west, are the unique Bahiri Caves (or Gadadecha Bahiri, as they are also called). Climbing up for 2 ½ hours from Saandshi through dense forest, we reach the valley and the slender mountain range of Kalkaray. From the valley, a small way towards the west takes us 150 ft down the plinths into the Bahiri Caves. One has to travel a very narrow pathway to reach the huge boulder which is the point from where we begin climbing. Finally, assisted by the natural vines and ropeways created by the villagers in that rocky terrain, we enter the Bahiri Caves. There are two caves, in which we can find a stone idol of Bhairoba (Bahiri) and a tank of cool water.

Whilst returning from here, one has to undergo similar 'exercises' to reach into the valley. But, instead of descending from the valley, take the pathway going ahead to Sahyadri range. There's a small climb to be conquered; having done which, we reach the Kundaleshwar (Kondeshwar) mandir (temple) in an hour's time. This is a very isolated and scenic spot. The small but picturesque temple, a small water body nearby and a clear starlit sky to give you company during the night, make for an enjoyable experience. If lucky, one can also spot a wild animal or two. A kilometre from this place is located the village of Jambhli, from where we can go via road towards Talegaon or Kamshet.

6. The Rocky Walls of Telbail and Scenic Ghangad

Whilst travelling on the Pali-Khopoli route from Konkan, the stony plinths of Telbail catch one's attention. In order to visit this naturally-gifted place, one can reach the Telbail village from Lonavala via road. If so inclined, you can also go into the valley. The dome-shaped temples located in this valley and the adjacent water body make you forget all exhaustion. The gushing wind and the faraway scenic view of Konkan is mesmerising. One gets humbled by nature's terrifying manifestation in the form of the two gigantic rocky walls. Those armed with adequate knowledge, practice and equipment needed for hiking are successful in climbing up these plinths to reach the peak via various routes.

> *One gets humbled by nature's terrifying manifestation in the form of the two gigantic rocky walls.*

Close to Telbail, is situated the small but scenic Ghangad. From Ekole, the village at the foothills of Ghangad, via the Bhambarde route, it takes around 1-1½ hours to reach the peak of the fort. Midway, one can visit the Gaarjai temple nestled amidst dense foliage.

A huge boulder on the peak of the fort, which has disintegrated but seems to be resting with its head on the fort's shoulder, is a prime attraction on Ghangad. An easy hike leads us to the peak of the fort.

There is a cave and a water tank on the peak. During the reign of Chhatrapati Shivaji Maharaj, Ghangad was used as a prison.

These are unique spots, ideal to be explored by a novice hiker – one who is willing to try a different route.

NASIK/SATAANA DHULE/AMRAVATI

1. Gaalna Fort

After the Setbari range of mountains on Sahyadri, towards the east, near Dhule, there's a chain of unusually-named forts on the Gaalna mountain range viz Dermal, Pisol, Kankrala, Lalinga, Bhaamer, Songir, Gaalna etc. In the 5th century, this area was ruled by Gavli Raja Veersen Ahir. Later, from the 16th to the 17th century, Mohammed Tughlak's general Malik Raza Faruki, established his rule here. After 1600 AD, the Mughal reign began here.

Gaalna stands at an altitude of 2800 ft.

On the Malegaon-Dhule road stands the village Dongrale and 2 km from here, is the Gaalna village, standing at the foothills of Gaalna fort. There's a direct ST bus from Malegaon to Gaalna. The 30-km distance can be traversed in an hour to reach Gaalna. In the village, there's a Nathpanthiya ashram. Close to it is a tiled road leading to the fort. Climbing up a small slope, we reach the east gate of the fort. The foundation and the doorway are in good condition. Inside, after a few steps, there's another doorway made of cast iron. There are small mansions towards either side of the iron door. Climbing up the stairs adjoining this door, one can go to the top. There's a wall to the left of the doorway near which is another small mansion and a tiger's sculpture. Climbing down the steps, one reaches the third huge doorway. Climbing some more steps up the left of this door, one reaches the fourth doorway. This doorway leads to the fifth doorway! Looking at the strong protective wall of the fort as is visible from here, as also looking at the structure and number of the stairways and doorways, one realises that most of the time, the enemy would have become tired of merely climbing up all of these, and have no strength left to fight.

Before the fifth doorway, one can see a pathway going towards the right. There's a ledge on the protective wall on the right. There are only two out of the four intricately carved pillars standing there now. Towards the right of this ledge, is another ledge; while towards the left are some caves. Further ahead is a mansion and a secret pathway. This pathway again brings you to the first doorway.

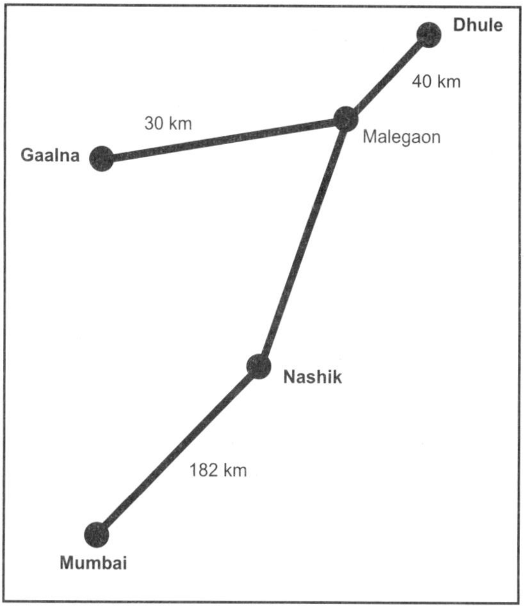
Dhule
40 km
30 km
Malegaon
Gaalna
Nashik
182 km
Mumbai

After the fifth doorway, we reach the peak of the fort. Towards the right, is a huge, rectangular water tank. Steps have been created to go down into the tank. Earlier, there was a temple on this fort devoted to Gaalneshwar Mahadev. Now, there's a dargah over here. There's a stairway to take you up the dargah. In front of the dargah, are the remains of two buildings with arches. Further ahead, at the north-west peak of the fort, is a bastion standing proudly with its beautiful arches and columns. On the plateau at the peak, one can see some seating arrangements and some graves. At a distance, one can see the Kankrala fort.

There are so many stairways that just climbing these would have tired out the enemy!

If you're carrying food along with you, the dargah is a good place to stay over at night; or else you can stay at the ashram at the foothills.

The distance from Malegaon to Dhule is 40 km. Malegaon-Nasik is 100 km whereas Malegaon-Gaalna is 30 km.

Gaalna was ruled by the Hindus, followed by the Nizam, Raja Bahirji of Baaglan, again the Nizam, then the Mughals, then Malharrao Holkar of the Peshwas and lastly, the British in 1818. Meandering over Gaalna and going over Garbad village, we can spot the 2476 ft high Kankrala fort. This is to the south of Gaalna. Apart from this, the 3500-ft high Pisol fort, Dermal fort and Bhamer fort are also located close by. One can visit all these forts in 5-6 days. Like the local language here, the names of the forts like Kankrala, Pisol, Lalinga, and villages like Lulla and Garbad sound amusing.

2. Lalinga Fort

The mountain on which Lalinga Fort is situated is very close to the highway while going from Dhule to Malegaon. In 1930, during Mahatma Gandhi's Civil Disobedience movement, there was a Satyagraha at the foothills of Lalinga. Lalinga village is 9 km away from Dhule. From the foothills the strong foundation, walls and other construction on the fort is clearly visible. One can reach the peak from the village in a mere half an hour. The fort is at an altitude of 1945 ft from sea level. While climbing up, one can see many caves formed in the foundation of the fort. One can see the main construction of this fort viz the arch at the peak, from way below the fort. Apart from this, there's also a pond, a few domes and a temple towards the west. Towards the right of the fort, is a water tank, beside which is a pathway leading to the *chor-darwaja* (secret door). Through this doorway, one can sneak down via the Dongrala route towards the Gaalna fort. Turning left from this place, one can see an underground three-mouthed cave! There's also a water tank close to this cave.

Ancient records mention the existence of two Hemadpanti temples on the fort but now no traces are to be found. The water tanks on the fort have been built 25 ft deep in stone. The tanks are perennially filled with water!

There's a bit of historical information available about Lalinga fort. When the Marathas defeated the Nizam in 1752, the Lalinga and Gaalna forts came to the Marathas as part of the treaty signed post-defeat. The Peshwas later gifted these two forts to Malharrao Holkar. In the Mughal era, Gaalna was a taluka.

Before all this, in 1437, it is said that there erupted a huge war outside Lalinga fort, between the king of Khandesh, Malik Nasir Khan and General Malik Uttujar of the Bahamani Empire. Nasir Khan was defeated in this war and had to take refuge in Lalinga.

One must visit this place as an important historical location near Khandesh highway.

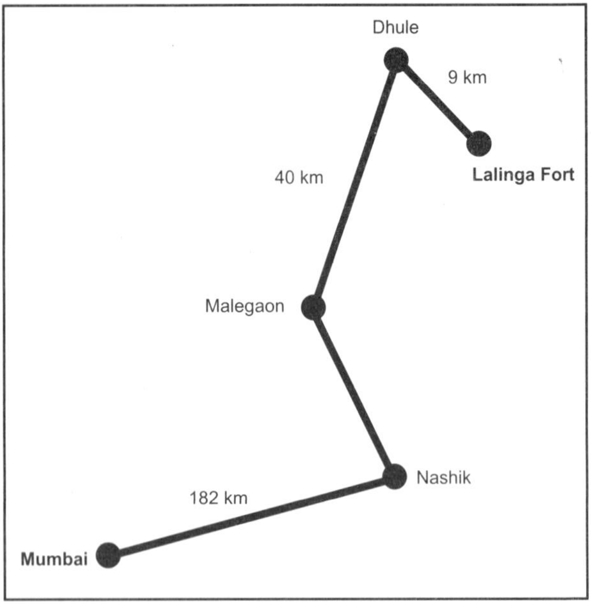

Lalinga Fort

3. Narnala

Narnala is counted amongst the largest forts. The area of this fort, located in Akola district and on the border of the Melghaat Tiger Reserve, is 382 acres. The fort has 67 bastions and 34 doorways. The fort at Jaffrabad in the east and Tojiyagad in the west is together called Narnala fort. The circumference of the protective wall around the fort is 26 km and the fort is located at an altitude of 3161 ft above sea level.

Since the fort comes within the aegis of the Forest Department, one is allowed to see the fort only till 6 pm. The fort is extremely huge and thus it takes 3 days to see it completely. For that, it becomes essential to trek up and down the fort every day. A pathway lined with white stone on both sides and going through a dense forest, takes you from the foothills to the main Shahnoor Door in 1½ hours. The door has glorious tiger sculptures on either side. Hence it is also called Sher Darwaza. There's also an 8 km long road to take you up by car. Entering through the door, one can see six slabs of stone. These are called as "Saha Gotyanchi Chhapri". On either side are two mansions. After that, one comes to the Mehendi Darwaza and the Mendha Darwaza. Then comes an intricately carved Mahakali Darwaza. There are two Bahamani inscriptions on this door. These inscriptions make a mention of the Bahamani Sultan Fateullah Imaad Ul Mulk restoring this door in 1487. After the Mahakali Darwaza, comes the fifth door through which we finally enter the fort.

The road, on which cars can ply, runs between the Shahanoor and Akot Darwaza and reaches the Shakkar pond. The entrance to the Shakkar pond is at the right. On the left, is the entrance to the fort. One can have a scenic view of the Shakkar pond through this doorway. This pond is perennially filled with water. It is said that if someone is bitten by a dog, a bath in this pond can cure him completely. There's a grave of Burhanuddin Awaliya. It is also called 'Kutardevache

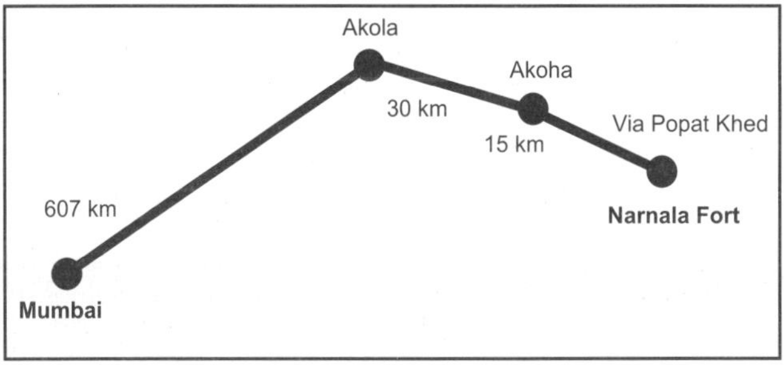

Thikaan'. It is a ritual to pray at the grave after bathing in the pond. After bathing and worshipping, one is not supposed to look back, all the way back to the foothills - or so it is said – to effect a complete cure. There's no scientific reasoning to support this belief but who can stop superstitions from proliferating?

To the right of the pond is the Rani Mahal building. This is a good place to stay during the day, because it is still in good shape. This place is also called Ambar Mahal.

Next to the entrance of Shakkar pond is the entrance to the fort. Though not much of it remains today, one can imagine its former glory even by looking at the ruins. There's a building to the south of this palace. Between these two lies the route to Tojiyagad. There's dense foliage all along this road and it is better to take along a guide. One can see a mosque and some ruins on this tapering end of Narnala. There are also a few small and big ponds in this part. Going ahead on a non-concretised road from Shakkar pond, one can see some parapets and the Ramtalav. Walking ahead from here one can see another pond to the left. There are arches constructed near this pond. Further ahead is a huge *naugaji* cannon (nine-yard-long cannon). This cannon was brought to the fort on the orders of Aurangzeb. There are two Persian inscriptions on this cannon. The valley seen beyond this cannon is called 'Chandan Khore'; because there are a lot of sandalwood trees here.

The fort was under the reign of Bahamanis, Burhanshahi, Nizamshah, Mughals, Marathas and lastly the British.

Akot taluka is located in the Akola district, 30 km from Akola. You can come upto this place by bus or car. Then, 15 km away one can come directly to Narnala via Popatkhed. A rest-house at the foothills provides good accommodation.

SHAKKAR POND AT NARNALA FORT: A DIP HERE OURES DOG-BITES

4. Gaavilgad

You must be aware of Chikhaldara. Close to it is Gaavilgad. According to the historian Farista, the Bahamani king Badshah Ahmedshah Wali built this fort around 1425-26 AD. Then why was it named Gaavilgad? Nearby, there was a fort belonging to a local king called Ahir, who belonged to the Gavli (cowherd) community. That fort was called Gavligad. Later, the name changed to Gaavilgad. In the 15th century, this was a part of the Bahamani kingdom. Soon after, the King of Ahmednagar won it. King Mohammedshah of Burhanpur tried to snatch it from him but he foiled the former's plans. Then, Akbar won it for himself. For some time after this the fort remained with the Nizams. Then, from 1636 to 1680 the fort was with the Mughals – much of the period during which Aurangzeb was the major-general over there. In 1680, Sambhajiraje and after him, in 1698 Rajaramji won over the fort with help from the Gond king. In 1803, the British General Sir Wellesly made a large-scale attack on the fort. Venisingh, a brave warrior put up a formidable resistance during this attack but sadly, he did not sustain for long. In fact, the British themselves praised his bravery. This fort, which has witnessed many important historical events, is awe-inspiringly huge. It can be viewed beautifully from the Devi Point of Chikhaldara and the Mozri point.

Gaavilgad stands 3600 ft high. The fort neighbours Chikhaldara, a hill-station in the Melghaat project region of Amravati. From the north, one can enter the fort through Machhli Darwaza. That leads to the second doorway called Beerbhaan. The third doorway, known as Shardul Darwaza, is 15-20 minutes away from the Beerbhaan door and is very huge. The royal symbol of a two-faced eagle known as Gand-Bherud is carved upon it along with a date tree. The pathway to this place goes through dense foliage. Climbing a few steps up from the Shardul Darwaza, one comes to the fourth doorway and then finally the fifth one, which is called Delhi Darwaza.

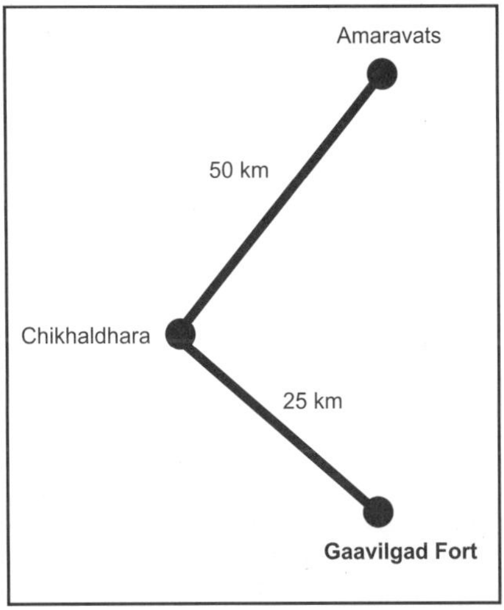

Just as Rajmachi was considered a focal point to keep an eye on Konkan from Pune, this fort was also considered important to keep an eye on Varhaad from Saatpuda. There are three big lakes viz Khaam Talav, Dhobi Talav and Dev Talav on the fort. There's a mosque on the banks of Dev Talav. Further on the pathway that runs between the Dev and Dhobi Talav, one comes across a temple. There's a bastion beyond this temple where a cannon has been installed. Nearby is the Kichak Darwaza. The ravine standing between this doorway and the Bhimkund point is called Kichakdari. There's a granary besides the Dev Talav. Further ahead is the sprawling Rani Mahal or Jama Masjid, as it is also called. The intricate carving on the entrance to this building is very beautiful. Going ahead from this point, one can see the southern bastion of this fort, which is called Bahram Buruj. A little away from there is the Mozri Buruj. Close by is the biggest cannon seen amongst all the forts of Maharashtra. It is 26 ft long. It is said, that there were 11 such cannons on the fort.

After this, one comes to the Fatte Darwaza, to the south of the fort. There's a holy shrine near this darwaza.

There are many wild animals, especially bears, to be found on the extensive plains of this fort. There are also other lakes such as Shakkar Talav, Machhli Talav and Kala Pani Talav on the fort.

There's a regular bus service to this fort which is 94 km away from Amravati. There are very good hotels and restaurants over here. Gaavilgad is a point in Chikhaldara itself. It is 2½ km away from Chikhaldara where one can stay.

5. Saalher

At the point where Maharashtra's northwestern border joins with Baaglan in Nasik and the border of Gujarat, the northernmost ranges of the Sahyadris are called Selvari and Dolbari. These ranges are spread in a long line across the Sahyadris' southeastern border.

In the Dolbari range is Maharashtra's highest fort and the second-highest peak amongst all the peaks in Maharashtra, called Saalher. After Kalsubai, which stands at 1646 m (or 5400 ft), Saalher stands at 1567 m (or 5140 ft). Towards the south stands the ravine of Mosam River.

Saalher also has a lot of historical importance attached to it. For many years in the 13th century, the King of Baaglan, Raja Maandev, ruled here. In 1639, the Mughals defeated Raja Bahirji and won the fort. They named it Sultangad. In 1671, Chhatrapati Shivaji won it back from the Mughals but soon again, in 1671 itself, the Mughals surrounded the fort with a huge army. Moropant and the Maratha general Prataprao took the Mughal army by storm and defeated it in no time. The battle was a gory one and the Marathas lost a braveheart called Suryaji Kakde.

Saalher also has mythological importance attached to it. Parshuram, in a bid to create new land, shot an arrow into the sea (present here) to make it slide back to expose new land – so goes the folklore. The gigantic footprints seen on the mountain, as also the huge hole seen in the opposite mountain, are proofs of this occurrence, say the villagers.

From Nasik, via the Sataana-Tahrabad route, come to Vaghambe, a village at the foothills. You'll encounter the Haranbari dam mid-way. From here, we reach the pass between Saalher and the neighbouring Saalota. One can climb the steps to reach the caves up here. It takes ¾th of an hour to reach the caves. One can go to the peak from here. However, if you come from Nasik via Kalvan and start climbing the carved-out steps from the Saalher village, it takes a mere half an hour to reach the first doorway of the fort. Beyond the first doorway lies a water tank and the second doorway. Then comes a third doorway beyond which is again a water tank and three consecutive doors. Going beyond these three doors, one sees an extensive tableland, called Gaadipathar. Towards the right, is the hill on which is the baalekilla (subsidiary fort). On the peak, is a temple devoted to Parshuram. This is the highest point of the mountain. Its kada (precipice) is as extensive

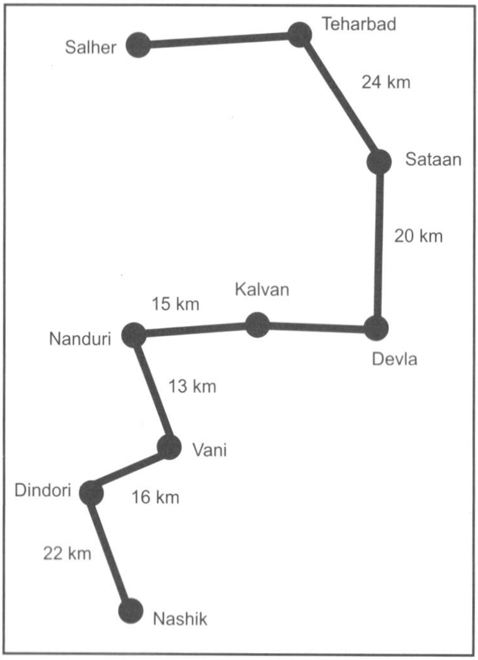
Teharbad
Salher
24 km
Sataan
20 km
Kalvan
15 km
Nanduri
Devla
13 km
Vani
Dindori
16 km
22 km
Nashik

Salher Fort

and dangerous as the Konkan kada of Harishchandragad. Since Saalher is the second-highest peak of the Sahyadris, one can see innumerable smaller peaks and a huge area of land, from this peak. Such a beautiful sight is visible on the Sahyadris only from select places such as Kalsubai or Kulang. Saalota, Tungi, Maangi, Mulher, Hargad, Dhodap Nhavi, these and others are visible from here. Amongst these, Saalota looks the most scenic.

Giant Footprints

On the left side of the peak, till the very end, are the remains of the protective wall of the fort. There's a small hillock on the peak. Before the hillock, on a tableland is a water tank, ledges and an altar for sacrificial rituals. There's also an idol nearby and a man-made lake. The lake has a huge pillar dug into it. On the right bank of the lake, is a beautiful temple dedicated to Devi Renuka. Every twelve years, the water of this lake turns milky; that's when a huge fair is organised here. Generally otherwise, hardly anyone turns up at this place, except for enthusiastic trekkers. Near the lake, in the belly of the hillock, are dug-out caves. There are quite a few small and big ledges in front of the lake. These might be the remains of old houses standing atop the hillock. Beyond this, is the western doorway of the fort. The way between the ravine on the left and the caves dug out in stone on the right, goes downward from the dug-out stairway, beyond two doorways. From here, we can again come to the Saalher-Saalota pass and descend into Vaghamba. One can return to Nasik in four days, visiting the main forts of Maangi, Tungi, Nhavi Saalher, Mulher and Saalota.

From Saalher village, one can go to the Chinchni village in the Dang area of Gujarat. You can return via the Ahva route. You can also come to Nasik from Saalher, via the Kalvan route. Saalher and the neighbouring places have a mélange of Marathi and Gujarati culture. The accent of the people here is quite amusing.

One can stay at the ashram (dormitory), temple or even at a villager's house at Saalher. Only, be sure to carry your own food and water.

6. Saamrad Saandan

A bewitching, small locale that can well be dubbed as Maharashtra's Grand Canyon, is Saamrad 'Saandan'. Saamrad village is located 20 km from the Shendi village towards the west of Bhandardara dam. From Saamrad, which ducks behind Ratangad and is flanked by Alanga, Madan, Kulanga and such other rustic forts, a 20 minute walk takes us to the entrance of Saandan. Saandan is actually a valley of pitch-black stony plinths that begins from the peak of the ghaats and descends down all the way to Konkan (in Karoli ghaat). To experience the grandeur and thrill of this ravine to the optimum, January and February are the best months to go; for, at that time, one can go deep into the ravine. There are quite a few huge boulders to be found in Saandan. As we descend deeper into Saandan, we get enveloped in an enigmatic, mysterious feeling. The minimum distance within this stony ravine is 2 km and the maximum is 30 km. While descending, one has to cross 2-3 ponds. As the slope of Saandan reaches its end, the size of the boulder reaches enormous proportions. One has to return to Saamrad via this same thrilling, risky route. If you take along a guide from the village, nearby you can also see a smaller version of the Konkankada of Harishchandragad. It takes around 4 hours to go from Saamrad to Saandan, view the place and return.

Ramdas Baande, guide - 9326673807

In Conclusion...

Indravejra — The Rainbows of Harishchandragad

Harishchandragad is the most distinct landmark on the border of three districts in Maharashtra — Thane, Pune and Nagar. It is adjacent to a prominent ghat section called Malshej ghat which is approx 2,300 ft. in altitude.

Harishchandragad is a huge mountain with a maximum height of 4700 ft. It has three pinnacles Harishchandra, Taramati and Rohidas. There are many caves, ponds and a 2000-year-old temple of Harishchandreshwar. But this mountain is more famous for a very unique cliff on the western side of the hill which is concave in shape and has attitude of 4000 ft. from sea level with a 1500 ft. straight drop. It is one of its kind in the Sahyadris.

There is one more mystical phenomenon experienced by many on this Konkan Kada, even by the Englishman Colonel Sykes in 1818.

During the monsoon when the mountain peaks are totally covered by clouds at the time of sunrise if you are sitting on Konkan Kada facing west you can see thousands of full rainbows with your own shadow in the centre.

FULL RAINBOWS AT HARISHCHANDRAGAD
A THRILLING OCCURRENCE ON KONKAN KADA

This can be experienced only for a few seconds and is difficult to capture on camera. The picture here was clicked by a trekker Swapnil Pawar.

Such and other enigmatic phenomena, many of which are still waiting to be unearthed in the remote corners of Maharashtra, add to the charm of the state. This book was an endeavour to showcase a handful of them.

I hope you've enjoyed reading 'Mystical, Magical Maharashtra' as much as I have enjoyed researching and writing it!

A TRAVEL GUIDE
OFFBEAT TRACKS
IN MAHARASHTRA
MILIND
GUNAJI